I HAVE A BURDEN

Greater Works than These. . .
Lord, Do It Again!

IRONSI JOHN

DEDICATION

This book is dedicated to God and to as many who are eagerly waiting for the next Mighty move of God on earth.

CONTENTS

DEDICATION
ACKNOWLEDGMENT
FOREWORD
INTRODUCTION

Chapter One
THE BURDEN UNVEILED
BASIC REQUIREMENTS FOR USEABLE MEN

Chapter Two
THE EARLY MEN: Reinhard Bonnke, Augustus Wogu, John Knox, Joseph Ayo Babalola, John G. Lake, Kathryn Kuhlman, Benson Idahosa, Smith Wigglesworth, Stephen, Aimee Semple McPherson, John Wesley, William Seymour, Elijah, Charles G. Finney, Oral Roberts, Maria Woodworth-Etter, Parham, Charles Fox and Evan Roberts.

Chapter Three
WANTED! WANTED!! WANTED!!!
Mantle Carriers…
REQUIREMENTS FOR ANY MANTLE

Chapter Four
SET US ON FIRE OH LORD
WHEN HE SENDS THE FIRE
IF WE MUST CARRY THIS FIRE
WAYS TO SUSTAIN AN IGNITED FIRE
HOW TO KEEP THE FIRE BURNING IN YOUR LIFE

EPILOGUE
OBITUARY OF UNCLE PRAYER
REFERENCE

ACKNOWLEDGMENTS

All glory to God for making this burden a reality. Daddy, words are not sufficient to acknowledge all that you are to me. I love you deeply and I owe you all.

This book, owes its existence to the encouragement and support I received from many people. I would be ungrateful if I did not acknowledge my indebtedness and express my heartfelt appreciation to some very special people. Regrettably, space will not permit me but I simply say to all whose names did not appear here. If you have helped or inspired me, you know yourself- thank you!

There are godly men and writers whose lives, messages and outstanding books helped in the making of this book: Apostle Anselm Madubuko, Pastor Benny Hinn, Rev. Dr. Chidi Okoroafor, Pastor David Ogbueli, Pastor Paul Enenche, Bishop David Oyedepo, and Pastor E. A Adeboye, Bro. GbileAkanni, Bro. Emma Okorie, Apostle Guillermo Maldonado, Rev. Dr. Mosy Madugba, Rev Sam Tukura, Apostle Joshua N. Selman, Robert Liardon, and so on.

Rev Samuel Onwere, Pastor Ochi Mark and Rev. Stephen Ezema (JP) I can't thank God enough for you, you picked me up and took me as your son at different stages of my life.

Thank you Rev Iyke Okoro, Rev Promise Dennis and Pastor John Jeremiah.

Thank you Rev. Abraham Chukwu for making time out of your tight schedules to write the foreword of this book.

My deepest appreciation to Esther, my only wife, best friend, lover, amazing mother, most faithful supporter and partner. You are truly God's gift to me. I love you.
To my wonderful children, Israel, Charis and Joshua, you guys are such a great delight to my life. Each of you is special and an inestimable treasure. Daddy loves you guys scatter.

Thank you world's best parents Engr. & Mummy Sunday E. Ironsi.

Thank you, Pastor Uchenna David Oliver for sparing your time to proof read this work.

Thanks to Engr. Dimgba Kalu. God made this happen through you.

FOREWORD

Every generation would usually have a catalogue of unannounced men; men who don't look like what they have gone through. These are men hidden in a 'closet' waiting for a time of divine announcement (1 Kings 19:18). They usually have no form or comeliness which inhibits their desirability for a time. But it appears to me that the more critical your assignment for the Kingdom, the more you go through things that are inexplicable but whose ultimate aim is to bring many sons to Glory. The only thing that keeps such men is The Burden laid in them by the Holy Spirit for their generation.

The Author; John Ironsi is a man I have known by the spirit to carry such a burden for this untoward generation. His personal testimony of salvation can ignite an unquenchable fire in your bones for right living. In this book, he has succinctly elucidated the spiritual characteristics of what I summarily christened as 'The Man God Must Use'. It is not enough to have a burden; you must make sacrifices to give expression to this burden.

God's method has been and will always be - A man! This book explores the life and times of such men who, in their generation, carried a burden and yielded themselves to God for divine expression. Their generations are yet to recover from their impacts.

I strongly recommend this book to every kingdom minded believer; your status notwithstanding.

Maranatha!

Pastor Abraham Chukwu
Lead Pastor,
Newlife Worship Centre.
Aba, Nigeria.

I HAVE A BURDEN

INTRODUCTION

God has planned from the beginning of the world to do all His works on earth through men. Man is a powerful tool God is willing to use to bring to pass His will on earth.

The scarcity of the power or move of God in our days is not as a result of deficiency on the side of God rather it is as a result of lack or unavailability of useable men.

"And I sought for a man among them who should build up the wall and stand in the gap before me for the land that I should not destroy it, but I found none."Ezekiel 22:30

No company runs her activities in isolation of her employees. No organization reaches her organizational goal or goals optimally without the working together or cooperation of her employers. **"The heaven even the heavens are the Lord's But the earth has He given to the children of men" Psalms 115:16.** The earth is God's company and the children of men are His employees.

Heavily built manufacturing companies do have in their list of employment men and women whose needs and concern arises when there is a breakdown. When something goes wrong or there is a breakdown somewhere these specialists will be needed around. In reference to these specialists it is their job to go into action to locate and fix troubled machineries and equipment. In the same vein, God at one point in human history shops for specialists whose chief concern or job is to fix cracks, breakdown, collapse and decadence in and around us, fix the mess of our society and the decline in the spiritual health of the church. But many times God looks for these men among men but can't find them.

This search for useable men is on even till this moment. The Lord is looking for men through whom He can display His extraordinary nature. He wants to do mighty deeds that will give witness to the reality of Who He is. Are you ready?

Holding and reading this book is a sign that there is a hunger in your heart to be used of God not merely occasionally, but consistently.

If we are going to do extraordinary things for God and with God, we must disabuse our minds from the Myth that you are too small and not qualify before God to make a difference. One man with God is majority and can make a whole lot of difference.

If one man, you or I can give ourselves wholly to God as we shall consider in this book, we will rise out of the ashes of mediocrity and ordinary and accomplished great things.

We can be used of God to heal, to make right wrongs, restore and rebuild broken walls, to unite that which is shattered, deliver those under oppressions, bondage and enslavement.

Long before I met the Lord and shortly after I came to the Lord, I heard and read about men who were extraordinarily and supernaturally used by God, people who subjugated kingdoms, shut the mouths of lions, quenched the rage of the flames and received back their dead raised back to life and I vowed to live a life different from the ordinary!

I did not want an empty powerless Gospel; I did not want to exist as powerless preacher of the Gospel of Jesus or representative of God. I desired the Acts of the Apostle kind of Christianity and ministry!

The question is; did God close His Acts (Mighty Works) with these men?

These men who out of obscurity; men who were utterly unschooled (Acts 4:13) shut down industries, Cities and governments just to score a point for the Kingdom of heaven. Men that changed norms, defile status quo, carried the Presence of God on a daily basis and off course decided how the earth and world at their own time tastes as salt and shine as light respectively.

It is evidently clear in some quarters, that the God of Glory or the Glory of God had departed, the salt has lost its taste, the gold has become dim, godlessness is prevailing, corruption, cultism and immorality is on the increase and God is saying 'I am looking for a man among them not an angel.'

Of reference to the man He is looking for; they are just common, ordinary men or a man willing and available.

Not necessarily those of the category of prophets, priests, kings and Leaders or ministry professionals. No!

God was and is still looking for those available not minding whether in the pew, the pulpit, the laity, the ordinary citizens or members of the public of the Church.

A collar around the neck or a piece of paper we call a certificate are not the things that endear a man to God.

Be patient with me as we journey through this book.

God has no other method but men; you and I!
Glory!
Are you ready?

IRONSI JOHN, 2020

HIGHER GROUND

1. I'm pressing on the upward way,
New heights I'm gaining every day;
Still praying as I onward bound,
"Lord, plant my feet on higher ground

Chorus
Lord, lift me up, and let me stand
By faith on Canaan's tableland;
A higher plane than I have found,
Lord, plant my feet on higher ground.

2. My heart has no desire to stay
Where doubts arise and fears dismay;
Though some may dwell where these abound,
My prayer, my aim, is higher ground.

3. I want to live above the world,
Though Satan's darts at me are hurled;
For faith has caught the joyful sound,
The song of saints on higher ground.

4. I want to scale the utmost height
And catch a gleam of glory bright;
But still I'll pray till rest I've found,
"Lord, lead me on to higher ground."

Johnson Oatman Jr. (1856-1926

CHAPTER 1

THE BURDEN UNVEILED

In every generation, for every age, the beginning of time, God seeks out for a man among men, unto whom He can commit Himself. Today more than ever we need men in our homes, communities and nations. Our people, families and the world at large has undergone and is still going through series of crises.

"God said, 'Let us make man in our image, after our likeness: and let them have dominion over the fish of the sea, and over birds of sky, and over the livestock, and over all the earth, and over every creeping thing that creeps on the earth. God created man in his own image; male and female he created them. God blessed them. God said to them, 'Be fruitful, multiply, fill the earth and subdue it. Have dominion over the fish of the sea, over the birds of the sky, and over every living thing that moves on the earth" Genesis 1: 26-28

Man was made in God's image. The word 'image' here is not referring to physical likeness, but is translated from the Hebrew words tselem and demut, both meaning essential nature, copy, characteristics and essence. This denotes that man as a spirit is an expression of God's moral and spiritual nature and attributes. In essence, man was created by God in the god-class and was given the responsibility to exercise that quality as God's agent on earth until the fall.

Ruin sets into human race as a result of the fall of man. After the fall, man was reduced to rubble and the natural or unregenerate man may barely find the faintest afterglow of that original holiness and glory that Adam once had.

As a consequence, marriages have collapsed, families broken and new generations emerge from the turmoil and confusion less able to grapple with the issues that face them. The restoration of man's broken image cannot be effected by institutions of higher learning, cannot be done by angels or money but by His Creator alone.

In God's rescuing and restoration process, He has no other method but men or a man! He has no other method to get things done on earth than locating a right and useable man. If there must be any intervention here on earth man must be involved. God is not ready or is He planning to use any other being on earth for these purposes except man.

Angels, as powerful as they are, will not even meet God's needs as far as the deliverance of man from sin and advancing the Kingdom.

The best animals no matter how strong they are or how much burden they can bear is not considered in this agenda.

Money, gadgets, houses etc God will not use. It is man that is God's instrument to accomplish His purpose. *"The heaven even the heavens are the Lord's But the earth has He given to the children of men" Psalms 115: 16.*

If it is in heaven the LORD is in full authority and His will is done perfectly; but the earth has been given to men by Him and whatever God wants to do here He needs to find a man to be His delegate and channel.

As we talk about men God wants to use, take your mind off from full time ministers and Pastors.

Being used of God is not synonymous only to full time ministers. A man may appear zealous and maybe had gone to theological seminary but God is not considering him useable.

God is in dire need of men. God's challenge in every age or generation is scarcity of men!

You may be wondering that the world is populated by billions of human being including so many designated men of God (MOG) yet we are talking about scarcity of men. In the days of Ezekiel God expressed such bewilderment loudly *"And I sought for a man among them that should make up the hedge, and stand in the gap before Me for the land, that I should not destroy it: but I found none". Ezekiel 22:30.*

What does God mean by saying that He searched for a man? What does He mean when He says He found none? How can you be searching for men when there are men everywhere in large numbers?

Did God not see all these men in the markets, offices, schools, churches, etc? God insisted that He found none, despite His strenuous search because He is not looking for just any man.

There are certain things He is looking for in the men He will use and He does not lower His standard for any man!

Even if a whole race is about to face destruction, the ever merciful God will still not act unless He can find the right man who meets His standards. Revival tarries because God has not found usable men.
How could God say this in a world that has literally over 7 Billion people?

How could God search for a man in a world with so many educated, talent men and claim to find none? What was wrong with all the men? These are some of the questions that run through my mind as I journey in life.

"I desired more than anything else to be used of God. The world is yet to see what God can do with, for, through and in a man who is fully and wholly consecrated to Him." D.L. Moody heard these words by **Henry Varley** over 150 years ago he determined in his heart to be that man! Moody gave himself fully to the will of God for and the Lord used him to shake two continents for Jesus. He preached to more than 100 million people during his ministry and many thousands came to know Jesus Christ as their Saviour.

Men God used in their times and dispensation were not super men!

Like Elijah, he was a man God sought and found. In our time God is saying I seek for a man regardless of his gender, race or human qualification or deficiencies that I may use.

Elijah we know was a man of like passion Apostle James said. In order words he is just the same as you and I. Elijah was not anything special to look at, maybe he wasn't anything special to listen to, he was a man of like passions like we are. He was subject to depression, he even ran away on one occasion from an ordinary heathen woman Queen Jezebel.Insert chapter one text here. Insert chapter one text here. Insert chapter one text here. Insert chapter one text here.

BASIC REQUIREMENTS FOR USEABLE MEN
It is now incumbent on us now to consider the condition of the man God will find useable. There are things that God looks out for in a man He want to use for this honourable course of restoring the dignity of mankind.

That you are a member of one denomination did not automatically qualify you for this noble purpose. This appointment is not done by man; the approval for this ministry is not made by human.

Lets draw scriptural analogy to appropriately deal on this matter; *1 Samuel 16:1 "The LORD said to Samuel, how long will you mourn for Saul, since I have REJECTED HIM AS KING OVER ISRAEL? Fill your horn with oil and be on your way; I am sending you to Jesse of Bethlehem. I HAVE CHOSEN one of his sons to be king."(NIV)* Saul's rejection is a matter of concern to me and then the choice of one of the sons of Jesse is a matter of serious focus also to me.

To God be praised that He did not reject the entire human race but just a man. So if He rejects a man another man can tickle His fancy.

"When he arrived, Samuel saw Eliab AND THOUGHT, surely the LORD'S anointed STANDS here before the Lord. But the LORD said to Samuel, 'DO NOT CONSIDER HIS APPEARANCE OR HIS HEIGHT, for I HAVE REJECTED HIM. The LORD does not look at the things man looks at. Man looks at the outward appearance, but the LORD looks at the heart" 1 Samuel 16:6, 7.

Considering the scripture before us and the drama that took place, I am always sceptical when people say to me 'The Hand of God is on you Pastor John…' wait a minute, before you conclude and approve Pastor John, what is God saying about Pastor John?

'…The LORD does not look at the things man looks at. Man looks at the outward appearance, but the LORD looks at the heart' the matter of the man God will approve for heavens use is a matter of the heart not appearance, not looks, not certificate nor height!

'When he arrived, Samuel saw Eliab AND THOUGHT, surely the LORD'S anointed STANDS here before the Lord. But the LORD said to Samuel, 'DO NOT CONSIDER HIS APPEARANCE OR HIS HEIGHT, for I HAVE REJECTED HIM'. For brother Eliab, I did not know how he appeared that day that even the renowned man of God, a prophet per excellent, a major prophet, the eye of God in his time was confused.

Enyi-my friend seek for heaven's approval. The man of God said '…surely…' meaning definitely, certainly, for sure, unquestionable, indisputably, categorically, absolutely, totally this is the man God delights in but lo and behold the man of God was wrong! Man can be wrong but not

Jehovah. Man is man; God is God!

"The eyes of the Lord search back and forth across the whole earth, looking for people whose hearts are perfect toward him, so that he can show his great power in helping them" 2 Chronicles 16:9.

So many of us are in the ministry, preaching, pasturing or doing one thing or the other in the name of the Lord over the years, I congratulate you and thank God for you. But I want you to press beyond people's appointment and applause so that your ministry can be confirmed by God.

Pursue God for endorsement of what you are doing for Him. When a man has got heaven's endorsement it does not matter where he stays.

No man in his natural state can fit into God's agenda. Every container He has used was formed, framed and fashioned from the dust of nothingness, world and self to fit into His mould.

Let's consider few of those things that can position a man to attract God to himself. Here are few of those considerations:

A MAN WITH NEW BIRTH EXPERIENCE

Brethren, church attendance, singing gospel songs, tithe and offerings, or being an active player in the church does not mean a man is born again. That you are even a preacher or officiate in the church does not make one born again. I remember asking a lady if she is born again. In her replies, she said, 'yes' and I asked her to tell me her experience and when and how the event took place. She said 'my parents are Christians, I was born in a Christian home and I go to church'.

Being born in a Christian home does not automatically mean that you are born again. That you are born in the parsonage, born by a minister of the gospel of Jesus Christ or pastor does not make one born again! Nicodemus was a highly regarded and respected minister in his day (a Pharisee and a ruler of the Jew), a faster and a tither yet Jesus made it clear to him that those credentials will not give him entry into heaven's service.

Jesus was blunt to let him know that: *"...Except a man be born again he cannot see the kingdom of God" John 3:3.* This is the first qualification of a man heaven must consider useable.

If you are not born again you can't fit into the mould of vessels God consider useable on this matter. When one is not born again, he has a nature and that nature is sinful. This fleshly nature must be discarded for the new one if a man must be used of God in this matter! When one acknowledges his sin, repents of them, trust and believe in his heart that Jesus Christ died for our sins, rose again for our justification and confesses Him with his mouth such shall be saved. You must ensure that your name is in this birth register to stand qualified to be used!

AVAILABLE MEN

Unfortunately some Christians are not at the disposal of the Lord. God uses people because they make themselves available – they yield to the Holy Spirit. God does not use people because they are perfect or talented, He uses people because they yield to Him. He is always asking: whom shall I send? That God uses men at all is a wonderful reality. From one point of view He doesn't need us. As Jesus once said, He could use stones if He wished, but He has chosen to use men. This means, of course, that He has chosen to use imperfect instruments. Yet our imperfection will not block God if our attitudes are such that we are willing to be used by Him.

If God must use us for His glory and lavish us with power from on high we must be placed absolutely at His disposal. God wants my yielded life. God wants your yielded life.

A BROKEN MAN

Brokenness doesn't sound like a sweet subject to talk about, but it is very powerful. It is one of the very important requirements for any man God will find worthy to use. It is one of the lessons you could ever learn if you want to be used of God. "When God wants to do an impossible task, He takes an impossible man, and crush him" **Alan Redpath.**

To be broken literally means to be shattered; to crumble and break into pieces for God to access. To be broken is to surrender your identity, self, pride, sinfulness that God may go through you or use you.

Unbroken men are like unbroken horses. No one can ride them and not even God can use such people. If God must use a man that man must of necessity be broken first. If God cannot crush you; you remain grossly unusable. "Unless a grain of wheat falls into the ground and dies, it remains alone; but if it dies, it produces much grain" John 12:24.

If you cannot die literally meaning; if you cannot be crushed by God you remain unusable. Too many of us are unbroken yet desiring God to use us. We have very few broken men!

Remember "...a broken spirit and a contrite heart, God will not despise" Psalms 51:17. God is looking for frail men into whom He can pour Himself, but crushing and brokenness process is so unpleasant that there are few candidates who want it.

A FULLY SURRENDERED MAN
One of the character accounts of any man God will consider useable is that he must be a fully surrendered man. Any life who desire to be used by God must belong to God.

Everything he is and everything he has must belong wholly to God. I am not saying that you must be perfect; you don't have to. If we are to be used in our sphere we must put all that we have and all that we are in the hands of God, for Him to use us as He will, to send us where He will.

ORDINARY MEN
From time immemorial God has been in the business of using ordinary men to do extraordinary things. The world, and sometimes even the Body of Christ, is impressed by people with wealth, fame, beauty, popularity, and high levels of education and accomplishment. Yet, these are not the criteria God uses when He calls people to be used by Him. He is not looking for those who are flashy, educated, charismatic, powerfully gifted, or highly accomplished to do His mighty works. Down through history, God has used simple, ordinary women, men, and young people who had a humble, passionate longing to be close to Him and were willing to do whatever He asked of them.

"God chooses things the world considers foolish, in order to shame those who think they are wise. And He chooses things that are powerless, to shame those who are powerful." 1 Corinthians 1:27 NLT

Disciples our Lord chose were uneducated fisherman and tax collectors. The members of the council were amazed when they saw the boldness of Peter and John because they knew that they were ordinary men who had no special training **(Acts 4: 13)**. He chose uneducated, simple people whom others saw as so insignificant.

Our Lord Jesus could have been born into an elite family of great influence. He actually could have come as royalty, and lived in an exquisitely beautiful palace, surrounded by extravagant comfort. Instead, Jesus chose to come into this world in a humble, darkened barn. It smelled of sheep, camels, cows and donkeys. There was only a dirt floor to lie down on, and there was no way to fill it with welcoming light or warmth.

David, the youngest shepherd son of Jesse became the giant killer and greatest king of Israel
God used Moses who was shy, fearful, and afraid to speak. Moses was also not the best speaker, saying, "Oh, my Lord, I am not eloquent, either in the past or since you have spoken to your servant, but I am slow of speech and of tongue" (Exodus 4:10), to which God replied, "Who has made man's mouth? Who makes him mute, or deaf, or seeing, or blind? Is it not I, the Lord? Now therefore go, and I will be with your mouth and teach you what you shall speak" (Exodus 4:11-12).

Smith Wigglesworth was an uneducated plumber. He couldn't even read. Nonetheless, he became an Evangelist who was powerfully used by God.

William Seymour was a poor, one-eyed, black man, with a severely scarred face. He was uneducated, totally unknown, and constantly up against the rejection that was part of being black in that era. Yet God used him to start the Azusa Street Revival that affected the whole world. This list goes on and on; God's will is to use ordinarily people like you and I because He is most glorified by this.

A MAN FREE FROM THE LOVE OF MONEY
This is the point at which many called evangelists and Preachers makes shipwreck, and their great works comes to an untimely end.

The love of money on the part of some evangelists has done more to discredit evangelistic work in our day. Loving money has cost some people their lives, lives of family members and of course their relationship with God. When one allows money becloud his visions. There is a tremendous difference between money and the love of money. A Christian can possess money but in a situation where money possesses a Christian it makes it dangerous.

It's was for love of money and material things that Gehazi, the supposed replacement of Elisha was denied the privilege (2 Kings 5). Instead of maybe double portion or triple portion of what Elisha was carry, he went home with leprosy. Heaven cannot lavish this solemn assignment of joining forces with Him in the bid to restore man to his original place on persons who are not free from the love of money

PRAYING MEN

Any man used of God had been a man of prayer. Any man that want God to be glorified in his life and ministry must be foremost a man of prayer. If you have not learnt how to pray, if you have not learnt how to wrestle with God then you do not want to have result in God.

HUMBLE MEN

"Faith gets the most; love works the most; but humility keeps the most." I believe God would use other men in a larger measure than I am been used. Oh, how many men full of promise and God used, and then abandoned and set aside because the man thought that he was the whole thing! I believe more promising workers have gone on the rocks through self-sufficiency and self-esteem than through any other cause. Oh, the men and women who have been put aside because they began to think that they were somebody, unknown to them that they were on "Industrial Training (IT)," and therefore God was compelled to set them aside.

Oh, men and women, especially young men and young women, perhaps God is beginning to use you; very likely people are saying: "What a wonderful gift he has as a Bible teacher, what power he has as a preacher, for such a young man!" Listen: get down upon your face before God. I believe here lays one of the most dangerous snares of the Devil. When the Devil cannot discourage a man, he approaches him on another direction, which he knows is far worse in its results; he puffs him up by whispering in his ear: "You are the leading evangelist of the day. You are the man who will sweep everything before you. You are the coming man. You are the Elijah, Apostle Paul of the day"; and if you listen to him, he will ruin you.

The entire shore of the history of Christian workers is scattered with the wrecks of gallant vessels that were full of promises a few years ago, but these men became puffed up and were driven on the rocks by the wild winds of their own raging self-esteem.

SEPERATED MEN

It is doubtful if there ever was a time when the note of separation is needed to be sounded more than today. The world has become so churchy and the church so worldly that it is hard to distinguish the one from the other.

The line of demarcation has been so completely broken down. Separation has always been God's standard. Abraham had to leave his country and his father's home and in complete separation to a place he knows not.

Moses refused to be called the son of Pharaoh's daughter. Separation is still the call of God. "Come out from among them and be ye separate, saith the Lord," and be ye not unequally yoked together with unbelievers" 2 Corinthians 6:14-18. The world must be forsaken and separation maintained.

A PREPARED MAN

The LORD said to him: "Before I formed you in the womb I knew you, before you were born I set you apart; I appointed you as a prophet to the nations (Jeremiah 1:5)." God knew Jeremiah; therefore He called him. It is that simple.

When God initiates a new ministry or work, He always prepares a man or woman and then works through that individual. God oversees the preparation for each person. The pattern is this: God makes the man; then the man makes the ministry; the ministry makes the church. But God always begins with a man. "The church is looking for better methods; God is looking for better men." This has always been the case.

We will not always be aware of our preparation. It seems sometimes that God delights in keeping us in the dark. Some of His best work occurs far from the prying eyes of men. Therefore God will never call upon us to do that for which He has not already prepared us. Trust Him. He knows what He is doing. Therefore, whatever opportunity that presents itself to us, as Christians we must believe that we have been prepared for it. The promise remains. "God's calling is God's enabling."

CHAPTER 2

THE EARLY MEN

We shall be considering lives, secrets and impacts of men and women that God found useable and how He used them. Men are powerful tools in God's agenda of restoring the kingdom. Our task and concern is to identify the way God is willing to use us to fulfil His mandate on earth.

There is no man on the face of the earth who lives such an unusual life as the man God would see fit to use for His glory and praise. If he is to be God's messenger, Christ's shepherd, the Spirit's vessel, then he of necessity must be an instrument prepared by the hand of God in any way needed to make it fit. God wants to use all of us it is important we note this truth. The reason God kept you alive is to be used for His glory. He wants your life to count. Our life is a lease. The reason God gave us this lease is to use us for His glory. He uses all kinds of people: sinners, the depraved, cheats, the rich and the poor, the powerful and the weak.

The term man is used in a generic sense which includes women as well. Man or woman, there is no respect of persons with God. God delights to use anyone, boy or girl, man or woman, who makes himself available to him. God chooses whom He wants to use; that is His prerogative. Our business is to make ourselves available; God's business is to choose. God uses people because they make themselves available. He is always asking 'who shall I send?'

These men and women we are about discussing here are not in its entirety complete list of men and women God used. There are countless numbers of them, that time and space will not allow me to discuss them all. So bear with me as we take these few.
Writing about these early men God used or found useable is not in any way to portray a special time and men God used and ends His need for men to use. Our intent for writing is to let you know dear reader, that it is now our turn and time. It is for us to know the extent God went with our fathers and assume our place in God. Take our stand for our generation and for our nations as we continue to duplicate, replicate the miracles of scriptures, interrupt and cancel funeral processions, take the light and truth found in Jesus Christ to our world, shut down wheelchair factories, struck terror in the heart of evil and enemies of our kingdom.

THE MAN REINHARD BONNKE
EVANGELIST AND PASTOR OF AFRICAN CONTINENT

Evangelism is the mission of the people of God (Matthew 28:18-20); and for God's people to carry out evangelistic work impact fully, words only are not enough! There is need for miracles and power to convince unbelievers. Like Apostle Paul, "My speech and my preaching were not in persuasive words of human wisdom, but in demonstration of the Spirit and of power..." Our words and preaching without power will only scatter what we were called to gather.

Power is the essence of the Christian witness. Christianity is either supernatural or nothing at all. Our Lord's ministry on earth for instance, operated in and with power and that enabled Him to performed many miracles. "...For this Man works many signs" (John 11:47). He opened the eyes of the blind (Matthew 9:27-30), unstopped the ears of the deaf, loosed the tongue of the mute (Mark 7:32-35), caused the lame man to leap as a hart (Isaiah 35:6) and raised the dead (Matthew 11:5; John 11:43, 44).

The Lord then promised His apostles the power to work miracles as they witness Him. "And as you go, preach, saying, 'The kingdom of heaven is at hand.' Heal the sick, cleanse the lepers, raise the dead, cast out demons..." (Matthew 10: 7, 8). He assured them of additional power. "Behold, I send the Promise of My Father upon you; but tarry in the city of Jerusalem until you are endued with power from on high" (Luke 24:49). "And being assembled together with them, He commanded them not to depart from Jerusalem, but to wait for the Promise of the Father, 'which,' He said, 'you have heard from Me... But you shall receive power when the Holy Spirit has come upon you; and you shall be witnesses unto Me in Jerusalem, and in all Judea and Samaria, and to the end of the earth'" (Acts 1:4-8). On the first Pentecost after the resurrection of Christ from the dead, the Holy Spirit came upon the apostles and gave them this power to work miracles and speak in languages which they had not learned (Acts 2: 1-11). "Truly the signs of an apostle were accomplished among you..." (2 Corinthians 12:12). "And through the hands of the apostles many signs and wonders were done among the people..." (Acts 5: 12).

"And this signs shall follow them that believe..."
Our discussion will centre on a man who discovered his evangelistic gifting and calling and stayed there. He did not deviate from it, or tried to become a pastor, bishop or general overseer. No, he started as an Evangelist and stayed so till the end. Quite unlike many of us today that never discover our

calling, or never stayed there because we want to become like someone else.

In 2013 he told some reporters that; "Some people call me a healing evangelist. I do not like that. I define myself as a salvation evangelist who also prays for the sick. Wherever we go, 95 percent of the meeting is a clear preaching presentation of the gospel."

ReinhardWilli Gottfried Bonnke Born on April 9th, 1940 in Germany, during the peak of World War II, was perhaps one of the greatest evangelists in the Christendom in the last two centuries, stepping into the shoes left behind by Evangelist Billy Graham and Evangelist Billy Sunday. The evangelistic campaigns of Graham and Sunday in America led millions to Christ. Bonnke took his campaign far in the dark continent of Africa where brutal and devilish traditions abound, where cruel human ruffians unleash terror on the vulnerable. With the Holy Spirit, his fame swept through the continent like wild fire, ushering millions of souls into the kingdom.

Evangelist **Reinhard Bonnke** the son of a pastor, gave his life to the Lord at age nine, and heard the call to the African mission field before he was even a teenager. After attending Bible College in Wales and his ordination in Germany he pastured a church and then went on to start missionary work in Africa. It was there, in the small mountain kingdom of Lesotho, that God placed upon his heart the vision of 'the continent of Africa, being washed in the precious Blood of Jesus'- an entire continent, from Cape Town to Cairo and from Dakar to Djibouti that needed to be reached and to hear the proclamation of the sign-following Gospel.

Bonnke ministry through Christ for All Nations (abbreviated CfaN), reached over 150 million persons with the gospel which more than 79 million people came to Christ as a result of these campaigns. His ministerial career, spanned from 1967 until his retirement in 2017.

Evangelist Bonnke began holding meetings in a tent that accommodated just 800 people, but, as attendance steadily increased, larger and larger tents had to be purchased, until finally, in 1984, he commissioned the construction of the world's largest mobile structure-a tent capable of seating 34,000 people! Soon, attendance at his meetings even exceeded the capacity of this huge structure, and he began open-air Gospel Campaigns with an initial gathering of over 150,000 people per service! Since then, he has conducted city-wide meetings across the continent with as many as 1,600,000 people attending a single meeting using towering sound systems that can be heard for miles.

After graduating from the Bible College of Wales and returning to Germany, Bonnke led a series of meetings in Rendsburg. He began receiving speaking invitations from all around Germany and the rest of the world. Bonnke met AnniSuelze at a gospel music festival, and admired the grace with which she recovered from a wrongly pitched music performance at the expense of losing the competition. He offered to preach at the church she attended one Sunday and fell in love with her. They married in 1964 and had three children.

As part of the discipleship-training program, 185 million copies of CfaN follow-up literature have been published in 103 languages and printed in 55 countries. Millions of books have been printed and freely 'seeded 'in nations around the world. All this is in addition to the Reinhard Bonnke School of Fire, an online, self-study course, aimed at inspiring others to Holy Spirit Evangelism and leading to either a certificate or university credits.

Reinhard Bonnke is also recognized for hosting 'Fire Conferences' in many different countries of the world, events that are aimed at equipping church leaders and workers for evangelism; for distributing over 95,500,000 copies of Minus to Plus, a profound salvation message, to homes around the world; and for seeking every opportunity to reach and to save the lost.

BONNKE saw in a five days crusade 9,120,000 registered decisions, people completing the decision card. "We counted the decision cards: 9,120,000 in five months. Next year instead of five crusades, I want ten crusades, and so instead of having 10 million, we will have 20 million souls for Jesus. In India, 1,200,000 persons assembled in a single meeting.

In one of his meetings in Nigeria, a man came back to life. This man was hit by a car. It was confirmed, he was stiff, rigor mortis and embalmed.

He had been embalmed but not with the removal of organs. They injected chemicals into the body to slow down decay, since there was no refrigeration.

His wife was one with a promise from God that woman have received back the dead by resurrection. She said, 'My husband will come back, and I have heard Reinhard Bonnke is in Onitsha this Sunday I will bring him there. She brought him there. I was preaching and I knew nothing about it. Suddenly, the man started to breathe"

God so anointed Rev Bonnke that most times as he steps on a platform, often without touching anybody, the blind begin to see, deaf ear are restored, the dumb start speaking and cripples walked. In his evangelistic ministry, miracles happened as if they were copied from the gospels and the book of Acts". In one of his meetings in Nigeria also, the crusade chairman in Onitsha, boosted "We know that when Reinhard Bonnke comes to preach, we will see the healing power of God in action".

At Bonnke's crusades each person at the crusade was expecting the miracle that would transform his lives; people look desperate enough to pursue it-to grab it by force if necessary... the healing power of God flowed each day as countless numbers reported evidence of the miraculous."

As beautiful as the results are it was not so from the beginning. Bonnke had a very rough Childhood. He grew up in an internal displaced people's camp. Early on, Bonnke encountered poor results from his evangelistic efforts and felt frustrated at the pace of his ministry. Reinhard Bonnke experienced a lot of setback during his missionary campaign in Africa. These setbacks, however, did not deter him from holding on to the promises of God for his life and Ministry. In the initial stage of his ministry in Africa, Bonnke experienced slow result in the pace of his ministry's growth. This setback left him frustrated.

When he started his ministry in Africa, he didn't get adequate support and cooperation from local ministers and churches. During one of his earlier crusade in Gaborone, Botswana, Bonnke rented an entire stadium but only 100 people were in attendance. These experiences were frustrating.

Bonnke could have given up on God and his ministry when the mobile structure he built to accommodate 34,000 persons was destroyed by the wind storm just before a major meeting. All these setbacks were not strong enough to sway him from the destination God intended him to get to. As Christians, we need to learn this virtue with him.

In 1974, Bonnke founded the mission organization 'Christ For All Nations' (abbreviated CfaN). Originally based in Johannesburg, South Africa, the headquarters were relocated to Frankfurt, Germany in 1986. This was done primarily to distance the organization from South Africa's apartheid policy at the time. Today CfaN has 9 offices across 5 continents.

Bonnke announced his 'farewell gospel crusade' to be held in Lagos, Nigeria in November 2017. Lagos is also the location of a gospel crusade held in 2000 which, according to CfaN, is the organization's largest to-date, drawing an attendance of 6 million people.

German evangelist Reinhard Bonnke, whose record-setting crusades led him to be nicknamed "the Billy Graham of Africa," was called home on December 7, 2019 at the age of 79 after a few battles with illness. Certainly a new chapter has opened in his life, a crown of glory which 'fadeth not away' from the Lord.

All told, more than 79-million people made Christ their Lord as a result of Evangelist Bonnke's ministry. It is no exaggeration to say that his work transformed our continent.

The life of Rev Reinhard Bonnke is good for those of us who are left and are still in the work of the Lord and carrying out our divine assignments, whether as Pastors, Apostles, Evangelists, Teachers, Prophets or as a member.

Bonnke said, the secret of his success is: "I have done nothing alone. God has called me and has been my pilot. The Holy Spirit has been my comforter, my guide, and my power source."

Evangelist Reinhard Bonnke was not after building the world's biggest or best auditorium for worship. He was not interested in amassing followers and congregation, neither was he interested in gathering wealth from the works of his ministry. His only passion was for lost souls.

THE MAN AUGUSTUS EHURIE WOGU
THE MAN BEHIND THE OLD UMUAHIA REVIVAL

Though in some quarters, the world is in deep slumber and God has not left her to sleep without warning. In the midst of the sleeping world some have been in every age awake. History must give credit to men and women who through their passion, daring faith, perseverance and unswerving commitment to faith, Pentecostalism was bred and nurtured in Nigeria. Pa Wogu is one of the unsung heroes through whom God birthed the revival movement in Nigeria and in extension the movement Assemblies of God Nigeria.

This piece contains not the story of the sleeping many, but one of the waking few. The world has written at large the history of church's sleeping multitude but our objective is to trace records of our fathers who God's mighty power raised.

Augustus Wogu formerly a member of Niger Delta Pastorate (now Anglican Church) was of Igbo descent and a native of Umuobutu in Old Umuahia in present day Abia State. Wogu later joined Faith Tabernacle and accepted the Lord under the Faith Tabernacle in the second half of 1930 while working in the Nigerian Ports Authority in Port Harcourt.

After his conversion, daily he engaged himself in house-to-house evangelism. Because of his radicalism in sharing his new found faith, news circulated among his kinsmen in Old Umuahia that he was mad. By January 1931, he paid a visit to his hometown in Old Umuahia following the biblical model (according to Acts 1:8) of beginning from one's home to witness for Jesus Christ, he went back to his village and preached Christ to his people. While at home, people watched him closely, instead of seeing an insane man as was rumoured, they were surprised when they saw a very sound and articulate young man. Due to his preaching, George Mnorom Alioha, Nathaniel Umechuruba, Marcus Asonye, Joseph Asonye, Abel Nwoji, Wilfred Woko, Godwin Akwarandu and many others were converted to Christianity.

The hunger in the hearts of these young converts, made them to read widely to increase their knowledge about God. Augustus and some of his converts devoted their time to reading religious literature that was flooding the country, especially The Pentecostal Evangel, a weekly magazine of the American Assemblies of God. Most of the literature they read carried stories of people who were baptized in the Holy Spirit, with evidence of speaking in tongues (in accordance with Acts 2:4).

About this time, the Pentecostal Evangel taught them about the doctrine of the baptism of the Holy Spirit. Armed with this knowledge they questioned their pastor in the Faith Tabernacle congregation about the baptism in the Holy Spirit and its attendant blessing of speaking in tongues.

After avoiding their questions on several occasions, the pastor eventually declared what the official position of the church was concerning the matter. When matters got to a head in a heated discussion with their pastor, they were asked to leave the church if they disagreed with the church's official position on the matter of baptism of the Holy Spirit. Thus in August 1934, the young men separated from the Faith Tabernacle congregation. They went home and established a prayer house where they met frequently to pray for the baptism of the Holy Spirit with Augustus O. Asonye as the first pastor.

Wogu and his group as they engaged in praying and fast, believing God for the outpouring of His Spirit. Then in September 1934, some of them including Marcus Asonye were gloriously baptized in the Spirit. As news of this experience filtered into Old Umuahia, their curiosity was heightened. Shortly after, the Old Umuahia brethren were also baptized in the Spirit. "That night before any sermon could be preached the Holy Spirit was poured out and many were baptised with the Holy Spirit and fire, with the evidence of speaking in tongues as the Spirit gave utterance. A revival had begun." and they received it (Alioha 1984:8).

After separating from the Faith Tabernacle congregation on account of differences on the matter of the Holy Spirit and speaking with tongues. They formed a congregation named it 'The church of Jesus Christ' (CJC). The CJC became zealously evangelistic and began to establish branches in the eastern, northern, western, and mid-western regions of Nigeria. The story establishes the fact that the Pentecostal outpouring in Igboland and Port Harcourt between 1931 and 1935 preceded the arrival of Pentecostal missionaries from America (Anderson 2007).

In the days following the outpouring, they engaged in intensive evangelism from house to house. As this happened, the converts that were won were baptised in water and in the Holy Spirit. Severe persecution arose from their parents and villagers alike. Married women were opposed by their husbands, and in some cases, they had their property confiscated. Many others were excommunicated from their homes.

Within five years of the revival, 15 churches had been planted. After 1935, the brethren began to pray for open doors to a foreign organization that shared similar beliefs they could affiliate with. They began to write to several Christian organizations in Britain and the United States. In June 1939, the American Assemblies of God sent a missionary and his wife, Rev. W.L. Shirer, who met with the local revivalists. Thereafter, in September 1939, they adopted the name, Assemblies of God Church Nigeria.

The beginning of the history of Assemblies of God Nigeria is traceable to this son of old Umuahia. AGN has experienced phenomenal growth as such that in 1959, the fellowship had 293 churches with 14,794 adherents. By 2013, this tally increased to over 16,300 churches and with over 3.6 million members and adherents. And all of this happened because someone whose name is now almost forgotten encountered the Lord and was hungry for the person of the Holy Spirit.

NOTE!

As Christians, we are supposed to have an impact on the world in which we live in. This book and examples of these holy men and women should cause us to think differently about how we can turn the world upside down for God. We don't have to live in the jungle in order to live radically for Jesus.

Today, men sets the rules, men determines what is right & what is not, men determines what they will allow God to do and not do. We are to an extent no longer the Church - we simply go through the motions of playing church. The church-world has become a dark wilderness -the Gospel message is diluted; true repentance is overlooked; total transformation has become a rarity; preachers, pastors and teachers rarely speak about sin, judgment, and hell - these are now big no-no's. Light a fire, Lord! Send us men like Wogu; burn away the hardness; burn away the immorality; burn away religion; burn away anything that hinders!

Until we as the true Church get tired of playing church, we will never break out of this dark wilderness we find ourselves groping in. You have to get tired of it all. You have to get tired of the ritual - the games - the carrying on - all the traditional junk. We have to come to the place where we find ourselves crying out in the wilderness for the fire of the Holy Ghost to bring a mighty change.

We urgently want and need men and women on-fire, red-hot, enthusiastic gospel advocator on this Earth! Believers who are DETERMINED to follow Jesus all the way because they know they have found the TRUTH! Such fervent Christians should all be driven by the same compelling COMPASSION which motivated the Apostles and the martyrs and virtually EVERY great man or woman of God throughout history! In fact, it's the same irresistible motivation that should motivate EVERY child of God in EVERYTHING they do, EVERYTHING they say, EVERYWHERE they go.

THE MAN JOHN KNOX
GIVE ME SCOTLAND OR I DIE…

Jesus Christ instructed his disciples in the Great Commission to "Go therefore and make disciples of all the nations…baptizing them…and teaching them." **Matthew 28:18-20.**

We the present day disciples of Jesus Christ who are keenly interested in obeying this commission should look back five hundred years to the time of the Protestant Reformation. This Reformation was not just a short time of revival, but it was an extended period of spiritual blessing that lasted approximately one hundred and fifty years in length. The burden in my heart is that God would bring forth another extended period of gospel expansion during our own era that the gospel will penetrate into many differing classes of people, some of whom had been largely ignored and brutally oppressed by religion, falsehood, materialism, and spiritual blindness.

Too many Christians and church leaders read books, go to conferences and get great visions of a church in their heads. But our problem remain, in some quarter, we don't have great visions for our communities. The truth here is that this part of us must have to die. Our own preferences have to be laid down to receive Christ's call and mission to our communities. I don't care what you like. As a church leader or as a Christian, you must be willing to die to your preferences so your community can be reached with the Gospel, and so must your church. Reaching a community for Christ is not about you and your preferences. It is more about Jesus and his mission to send you to people. Until the church dies to its comfort, luxury, preferences, wants and desires, it will not be able to reach the community. But like a grain of wheat, it must die so that it may bring new life.

John Knox, the most famous Scottish Reformer and founder of Presbyterian Church was among a number of key men God raised-up who rediscovered the gospel during the Reformation and widely taught it throughout Europe. The rediscovery of the gospel brought about a renewed interest in the Bible and as a result Europe was plunge out of its extended period of spiritual darkness into the light.

Knox was born in the family of a middle-class farmer in Southern Scotland in the year 1514. John's father was not well off, he did have enough money to send him to study at St. Andrews University. It was planned by his father that John would become a priest in the Roman Catholic Church. At St. Andrews, John studied under a well-known critic of the Roman Catholic Church, **John Major** 1467-1550.

In his lectures, Professor Major encouraged the return of the Roman Catholic Church to a simplified form of ecclesiastical government, which he argued was practiced by the New Testament Church. Church leadership was to be in the hands of the local elders and deacons and only when there were weightier matters to resolve were these men gathered together into presbyteries and synods.

John Major had a powerful impact on the bright young Knox, exposing him to many of the arguments supporting the growing reform movement.

Knox returned to Scotland, only to be driven out by persecution the next year. Returning to Geneva, Knox accepted a call to pastor the English church there. During this time, Knox offered his best-known contribution to the Reformation. Until Knox, and for some time afterward, the Reformers believed that a Christian must always live in submission to secular authorities. From **Romans 13**, they reasoned the King (or Queen) was established by God and, therefore, must be obeyed. Even wicked monarchs were to be obeyed, insofar as their commands didn't violate Scripture. For Knox, this unquestioning obedience was unacceptable.

Nevertheless, upon his graduation from St. Andrews University in 1540 Knox followed the wishes of his father and took up orders as a Roman Catholic priest. In addition to his priestly duties, which were few, Knox also served as a Papal notary authenticating legal documents. In many respects, Knox had accomplished all that his earthly father had dreamed about for his son: he had the endorsement of the church, the prestige of higher education, and sufficient money from his work as a notary. However God, his heavenly Father, would not let John Knox be content with all of his worldly accomplishments, but would instead, draw him to a living faith in Christ.

At the time of John Knox's ordination in 1540, King Henry VIII (1491-1547) ruled England. Against the wishes of the Pope, Henry divorced his first wife, Catherine of Aragon and started his own national church, the Church of England. Without really knowing it, Henry had aligned England with the Protestant cause. As to religion, the popular maxim of the age was this: "As the King believes, so does the nation". Thus, England became a country where Protestant ideas were tolerated within the framework of the Anglo-Catholic theology of the Church of England. The Scottish lands, on the other hand, were separated from England politically and ecclesiastically being ruled by Roman Catholic monarchs. As a result, the growth of Protestant ideas in Scotland was often regarded as rebellion against the political authorities. Scotland seemed destined to remain Roman Catholic, unless, of course, God raised-up a champion of the Protestant cause in Scotland.

Focusing upon the Old Testament, Knox came to a different conclusion. Central to Knox's position were the prophets and their insistence upon purifying the nation of Israel from idolatry. For Knox, the implications were obvious: just as Christians could not obey wicked laws, they should not submit to wicked rulers. In his mind the Catholic Mass was idolatry, and therefore, the Catholic was an idolater. Any Catholic monarch—such as Queen Mary I—was, therefore, an idolatrous and wicked ruler. Christians should not submit to such rulers but oppose them.

Returning to Scotland in 1559, Knox led the Reforming party of Scotland. He continued to promote reformation and raised troops to assist in that goal. Over the last thirteen years of his life, Knox passionately fought for reform in Scotland and opposed the Catholic Church and Catholic rulers.

Knox is remembered as a firebrand Reformer who was either loved or hated. But his greatest legacy may not have been the Scottish Reformation. By arguing for rebellion, violent if necessary, against wicked rulers, Knox laid a foundation upon which others would build. His thinking about the relationship between God, the Sovereign, and the Subject, though extreme for his day, was means to what became the American Revolution. Without John Knox and his influence upon later men such as Thomas Jefferson and Patrick Henry, it is possible the American Revolution would never have occurred.

When Knox returned to England he was offered a position as preacher at Berwick in northern England. Knox's unwavering commitment to the pure preaching of the gospel was a bright and shining light amid the darkness in a nation steeped in doctrinal and ecclesiastical compromise. Knox was a committed pastor and churchman whose ministry served as a compass to numerous pastors. Several years of fruitful ministry followed and he became well known throughout England as a great preacher. Knox did not fear any man, because he feared God—he was a man willing to offend men, because he was unwilling to offend God. People fear John Knox, not because of his sword, but because of his words. Knox was a bold preacher of the Bible and its message of liberty in Christ.

When Mary I (1516-1558), the infamous "Bloody Mary", came to power in 1553 after the untimely death of Edward VI many Protestant leaders had to flee for their lives. Queen Mary I was determined to restore the Roman Catholic faith to England and sought to accomplish this through the severe persecution of Protestants. Under her reign such notable reformers as Thomas Cranmer, Nicolas Ridley, and Hugh Latimer were executed.

For six long years Mary and John Knox battled with a war of words that occasionally broke over into violence. Specifically, Knox felt that Mary's celebration of the mass in her private chapel was idolatrous and in violation of the second commandment (Exodus 20:4-6). Also, she affirmed the "divine right of Kings" (i.e. that God had given her authority over the

Scottish people) which Knox felt was in violation of the "divine right of the people" (i.e. to have a Queen who was submissive to God and to biblical law). His controversial tract "The First Blast of The Trumpet against the Monstrous Regiment of Women" delivered a boiling criticism against the woman rulers of his day each of these women Knox identified as "Jezebels."

John Knox preached and prayed to the end that God would rescue Scotland precisely because he was clinging to Jesus' promise and prayer to save His people from every tribe, tongue, and nation. It should be no surprise to us then that when Knox was near death, he asked his wife to read to him the High Priestly Prayer in John 17 that our Lord Jesus prayed the night before He went to the cross. Knox called this passage "my first anchor." Christ is the captain of our souls, the anchor and only hope of the nations. Therefore, in light of so great an example of God's power working through one man, let each one of us pray with the same passion for our nation—and all nations—as Knox prayed for Scotland.

Knox's prayer was not an arrogant demand, but the passionate plea of a man willing to die for the sake of the pure preaching of the gospel and the salvation of his countrymen. Knox's greatness lay in his humble dependence on our sovereign God to save His people, revive a nation, and reform His church. As it is evident from his preaching and prayer, Knox believed neither in the power of his preaching nor in the power of his prayer, but in the power of the gospel and the power of God, whose sovereignty ordains preaching and prayer as secondary means in the salvation of His people.

Knox's major contribution to the Reformation and to Western Civilization was his teaching on the legitimacy of resistance against tyranny. Knox was not a revolutionary, however, as his life and sermons prove. It was this kind of practical application of the Bible's teaching that resulted in the rapid progress of liberty throughout the Western world. Evil and tyrannical governments were resisted and thrown off in Scotland, England, France, Germany, Holland, and in the American Colonies. Other theologians who came later would further develop Knox's ideas, but the original seed came from Knox as he struggled with how to bring religious liberty to Scotland, his own beloved country.

Perhaps more than anything else, John Knox is known for his prayer "Give me Scotland, or I die." As said earlier Knox prayer was not an arrogant demand, but the passionate plea of a man willing to die for the sake of the pure preaching of the gospel and the salvation of his countrymen.

Although Knox was imprisoned, enslaved, and persecuted, he consistently lived out his theology, believing that "one man with God is always in the majority." As such, the prayers of one man heard at the throne of God were a threat to the throne of Scotland!

At his funeral, in November 1572, the newly appointed Regent of the Scottish government gave this glowing testimony of Knox: **"Here lies a man, who in his life never feared the face of man; who hath been often threatened with dagger, but yet hath ended his days in peace and honour."**

The legacy of John Knox lives on, if not in Scotland, then throughout the world where the gospel is believed, preached, and taught.

Though Knox remains a paradox to many, he was clearly a man of great courage. Knox wasn't afraid to stand up to anyone, even kings and queens, for what he knew were right. His preaching was used by God to transform the whole of Scotland. Knox's legacy is large: his spiritual progeny includes over 750,000 Presbyterians in Scotland, over 3 million in the United States, hundreds of thousands in Nigeria and many millions more worldwide.

I would not want you remain the same before picking and reading this book. We must prepare our hearts to experience the fire that burnt in these lives. Our world is headed towards hell, our generation is under a serious attack, sin, wickedness, corruption, and compromise, immorality is on high rate; it is time we rise.

The needs of the hour is men like John Knox; on-fire, red-hot, enthusiastic, who love the Lord more than anything or anyone else on this Earth, men and women who neither will be flattered nor fear any flesh, men and women who in their lives will never fear the face of man. Wanted disciples who are DETERMINED to follow Jesus all the way because they know they have found the TRUTH!

Men and women who NOTHING could quench their enthusiasm about their revelation and conviction of who the Lord is, just like Paul; *"Five times I received from the Jews forty lashes minus one. Three times I was beaten with rods, once I was stoned, three times I was shipwrecked, I spent a night and a day adrift in the open sea, I have been constantly on the move. I have been in danger from rivers, in danger from bandits, in danger from my own countrymen, in danger from the Gentiles; in danger in the city, in danger in the country, in danger at sea; and in danger from false brothers! I have labored and toiled and have often gone without sleep; I have known hunger and thirst and have often gone without food; I have been cold and naked."* *2 Corinthians 11:24-27*. Apostle Paul never let these difficulties and obstacles stop him. In same way John Knox went right on serving God no matter WHAT hardships or difficulties befell him!

Wanted! Wanted!! Wanted!!! Uncompromising Christians who will preach pure gospel of our Lord Jesus Christ no matter what hardship or difficulties they face or meet!

Sadly today in some quarter, most in 21st century Church and Christianity, the fire has long been extinguished. For many of us Christians, we are as cold, indifferent, dead, formal, usual, and even irrelevant to their everyday lives and in our society. I hope you agree to an extent. Many of us and churches are more like fridges than baking oven. Many places of worship are more like mortuaries than Centres of new life. **I want to challenge you today individually and as a church, let's take our nations for Jesus Christ!**

THE MAN APOSTLE JOSEPH AYO BABALOLA
THE FOUNDER OF CHRIST APOSTOLIC CHURCH (CAC)

Joseph Ayo Babalola lived from 1904 to 1959. Apostle Ayo Babalola is one of the greatest men of God that have ever treaded the face of this earth. He was one of the first sets of prophets God used to lead a great revival in Nigeria.
Ayo Babalola was born on the 25th of April 1904 at Odo-Owa,Ilofa, in present day Ekiti Local Government areas of Kwara State, Nigeria. His parents, Pa David LawaniRotimi and Madam Martha TalabiRotimiwere devoted Christians and were also the founder of CMS church at Ilofa/Odo-Owa.

Papa Ayo was taken to Lagos by his Uncle, Mr. M.O. Rotimi who was a teacher at C.M.S. He went to elementary school at Oto-Awori near Badagry before he went to Methodist school at ago ijaye in EbuteMetta Lagos for just 2 years before he was enrolled again at All saint M.C.S school in Osogbo, Osun State where he studied in Nigeria Reader IV (primary 4) and he stop his education to learn Blacksmith for two years.

He also learnt Roller Driver under P W D (Public Works Department), he became a Steamroller Operator then under the control of the whites. After

15 days of learning how to drive the caterpillar, he was able to drive it without any assistance. After nine months; he became a master in his class.

Babalola's strange experience started on the night of September 25th, 1928 when he suddenly became restless and could not sleep. This went on for a week and he had no clue of the cause of such a strange experience. The climax came in October 9th 1928 about 12.00 noon. When suddenly the steamroller's engine stopped to his utter amazement, there was no visible mechanical problem, and he became bewildered and confounded.

He was in this state of bewilderment when an enormous voice "like the sound of many waters" called him three times saying "Joseph! Joseph!! Joseph!!! The voice was loud and clear and it told him Leave this job you are doing; if not, this year you are going to be cut off from the earth." Again on 11th October 1928, while trying to repair his machine, he heard an audible voice from the Lord to abandon the job and start preaching. That was how he received the call and he went into fasting and prayer. During this period of fasting and prayers, he received lots of revelations which formed the basis of the way he operated in his ministry. He later joined the Faith Tabernacle Church in November 1929 where he was baptized in Lagos lagoon in December the same year.

Papa Joseph Babalola became a prophet and a man with extraordinary powers. Enabled by the power of the Holy Spirit he could spend several weeks in prayer.

Following the voice of the Lord that Apostle Babalola heard in 1928, his first miracle was when the revival of his mission began with the raising of a dead 10 years old boy in September 1930. What followed this in three weeks was the healing of about 100 lepers, 60 blind people and 50 lame persons. This also resulted in the desolation of Churches in Ilesha because their members transferred their allegiance to the revivalist and that all the patients in Wesley Hospital, Ilesa, abandoned their beds to seek healing from Babalola. This divinely kicked off The Great Revival of 1930, which saw people coming from most parts of Africa and Diaspora without posters and TV adverts.

This Great Revival of 1930 shook Nigeria's social, economic, cultural and religious structures to its foundations. Close to 2 million people witnessed the Revival in Ilesha." Babalola's stoic simplicity and single minded dedication to his calling remain unparalleled in these times of indefensible compromises; he was a Christian revivalist, given to aggressive proselytization of the word of God, faith healing and miracles. It has been documented for example, that at least 15 stone dead people came back to life in Babalola's revivals.

He toured Yoruba land and eastern Nigeria, preaching about repentance, and renunciation of idolatry, the importance of prayer and fasting, and the power of God to heal sickness. And all through his tour, he has with him, his bell and Yoruba Bible in his hand. During this period he also visited many towns and villages based on the Lord's guidance where he preached the message of healing and deliverance to the people. However for a period of six months he still maintained a strict regime of prayer and fasting.

The watershed in his early ministry came when he was commanded by God to go to his hometown to warn his people against Idolatry, fetish practices and evil works. According to him, he was told to go to his hometown, where he was born. The Lord said I should rub my face with ashes and to carry palm leaves in my hand and to buy a bell, which I was to be ringing the moment I entered the town and I obeyed. The voice told me to tell my people that unless they repent, evil beasts would enter the town to destroy them. On that same day I entered the town with a bell in my hand. The entire town was moved and there was great stir and anxiety as people fled as they saw me.

The moment they set eyes on me they fled. The Voice told me to ring the bell in my hand round the town and I obeyed. His people however refused to repent or change their ways they instead summarily beat him up and his family was subjected to heavy persecution by the people of the town. In defence against the prophesied invasion of the town by wild beasts the people of the town armed themselves with Guns and Cutlasses. However God told His Servant to tell them he would not bring beasts again but instead would bring epidemics and it would start within forty- five days. At the expiration of the prophesied forty-five days and epidemic of small pox broke out and within 3 weeks about 300 persons had died. But those who repented and those who came to the man of God after contracting the disease were spared.

Another fact about him is that, Apostle Babalola will pray for days nonstop. According to some of his disciple that said, on several occasion he prays to God on broken glass. He also sometime stand for 7 days praying to God nonstop. Another interesting scenario of his prayer style is that Babalola's shortest and brief prayer was that of 3 to 4 hours. He was a prophet and a man with extraordinary powers enabled by the power of the Holy Spirit. Ayo Babalola was later sent out of the Anglican Church of his village by his Bishop because most members of the Church see visions; speak in tongues and pray vigorously.

Babalola was a spiritually gifted individual who was genuinely dissatisfied with the increasing materialistic and sinful existence into which he believed, the Yoruba in particular and Nigeria in general were being plunged as western civilization influence on society grew. The C.A.C believes that the spiritual power bestowed on Babalola placed him on an equal level with Biblical apostles like Peter, Paul and others who were sent out with the authority and in the name of Jesus.

He was one of the first and few prophet of God that have the grace to know when they will die, as he predicated his death in 1957 for his disciple at ikere Ekiti during his 3 days fasting and prayer with them.

Babalola's evangelistic success in Efon-Alaaye was a remarkable one. Archdeacon H. Dallimore from Ado-Ekiti and some white pastors from Ogbomoso Baptist Seminary were believed to have come to see for themselves the "wonder-working prophet" at Efon. The success of the revival was accelerated by the conversion of both the Oba of Efon and the Oba of Aramoko. They were both baptised with the names, Solomon AladejareAgunsoye and Hezekiah Adeoye respectively.

After this event, news of the revival at Efon spread to other parts of Ekitiland.

The Muslims in Offa became jealous and for that reason incited the members of the community against him. To avoid bloodshed he was compelled to leave. He stopped next at Usi in Ekiti land for his evangelical mission and he performed many works of healing.

Joseph Babalola requested an open space for prayer from the Oba who willingly and cheerfully gave him the privilege to choose a site. Consequently, the prophet and his men chose a large area at the outskirts of town.

Traditionally the place was a forbidden forest because of the evil spirits that were believed to inhabit it. The Oba tried to discourage him and his men from entering the forbidden forest, but Babalola insisted on establishing his prayer ground there. The missionaries entered the bush, cleared it and consecrated it as a prayer ground. When no harm came upon them, the inhabitants of Efon were inspired to accept the new faith in large numbers. Joseph Babalola's evangelistic success in Efon-Alaaye was a remarkable one.

One Mr. Cyprian E. Ufon came from Creek Town in Calabar to entreat Babalola to "come over to Macedonia and help." Ufon had heard about Babalola and his works and wanted him to preach in Creek Town. After seeking God's direction, the prophet followed Ufon to Creek Town. His campaign there was very successful. From Creek Town, Babalola visited Duke town and a plantation where a national church existed at the time. Certain members of this church received the gift of the Holy Spirit as Babalola was preaching to them and were baptized.

The following year Apostle Babalola, accompanied by Evangelist Timothy Bababbusuyi, went to the Gold Coast. On arrival at Accra, he was recognized by some people who had seen him at the Great Revival in Ilesha. After a successful campaign in the Gold Coast he returned to Nigeria.

In 1959 Apostle Joseph Ayodele Babalola eventually slept in the Lord, after a glorious and remarkable revival he incurred in Nigeria. **"Apostle Babalola said the reservoir of prayer he had prayed was enough to be raising up men and women to evangelize the nation till the Second Coming of the Lord Jesus Christ and today we can behold the effect of his divine prayers in Nigeria today.**

NOTE:
The Lord desires to do greater and mightier things in and through us. He longs for it. He wants it. He promised it and He is ready to do it. God wants to do even in greater measure what He did in and through these early men.

God has promised to do His own part. The problem is that we have often failed to pray; we are weak in prayers. The man who prays will have the promises of God fulfilled in his life and time. We don't do what these had done because we don't pray or had not prayed. We don't get results because we don't pray. We need to hold on to God persistently, fervently and effectually as we ought to. God is calling us back. If we want the same experience these men and women had in their days, repeat itself in our days, lives, families, churches and ministries, we must get back to the place of prayers. This kind of anointing does not come by folding of hand but by prayer, prayer, prayer and fasting.

Are we not like a God-forsaken land? How can we explain our state; unbelievers attend our meetings and go home the same smiling and untouched, unbelievers come into our gatherings and steal phones, bomb churches, kidnap members and go scot-free? Such could not happen in the days of these early men. God is calling us back to Himself, who will resolve to answer His call?

THE MAN JOHN G. LAKE
A MAN OF HEALING

The story of John G. Lake is one of incredible displays of God's power and divine provision. His life is arguably had one of, if not the most dynamic gifts of healing of any revivalist in human history.

The will of God in this generation is to raise from amongst us combustible vessels who will carry such healing anointing and grace. John 14, *"Truly, truly, I say to you, whoever believes in me will also do the works that I do; and greater works than these will he do, because I am going to the Father."* We cannot be really called God's people if we cannot manifest and demonstrate God to our generation.

More than ever in the history of man, God is willing and eager searching for willing hearts to demonstrate His power through. We have not in full capacity maximized all that God has for us. In other words, we are half way to the availability of all that God has for us. What we are talking about here is not for the hierarchy of the church. No! It is available to all willing hearts. It is available for you.

John G. Lake was not such an idol; he was an ordinary man who obeyed the voice of the Lord in radical and unprecedented ways. He was nothing special, a normal guy who simply laid it all down for the glorious gospel. Despite the faith in which Lake walked, he was far from perfect. In fact, he made some critical mistakes that any God fearing follower of Jesus would vow not to make. Allow this story to provoke you into faith and courage to embrace the cost of integrity, honour and excellence.

If there was ever a man who walked in the revelation of "God in man," it was John G. Lake. A man of purpose, vision, strength and character, his one goal in life was to bring the fullness of God to every person. He often said that the secret of heaven's power was not in the doing, but in the being. He believed that Spirit-filled Christians should enjoy the same type of ministry Jesus did while living on earth, and that this reality could only be accomplished by seeing themselves as God saw them. John G. Lake lived his life and fulfilled his ministry on earth with this type of spiritual understanding. If we would just grasp the reality of our position through Jesus Christ, as Lake did, every nation would ring with the praises of God.

John Graham Lake was known as God's "Apostle to Africa". He was born in Ontario, Canada on March 18th, 1870. He was a family man, person of integrity, honour, a confidence businessman and a good father. If you knew him you wouldn't otherwise know that he would soon become one of the greatest men of God the world would ever know. He had a genuine love for the Lord Jesus and was known by his friends as a man who dedicated himself to intimacy with The Lord.

By 1905, John G Lake was making $50,000 per year this sum would be like upwards of 182, 550, 000 naira per year annually at 1 dollar for 365 naira. John grew up in a family environment which was plagued with sickness and death, it is said that his earliest memories were of sickness, death and funerals. He was from a large family; he had 16 siblings, 8 of which tragically died of various diseases. It is no coincidence that "the man of healing" was tormented from a young age with death and disease. The enemy will often oppose destinies with radical circumstances through a distortion of the very thing that we are called to walk in.

Lake was exposed to dramatic healing when he visited John Alexander Dowie's ministry. While praying, he was instantly healed of rheumatism which had caused his legs to grow incorrectly. Lake felt a call to the ministry, and studied to become a Methodist minister. He took to heart the Methodist teaching on sanctification and sought it passionately. When his studies were done, however, he made a decision to go into business and start a newspaper in Illinois. Then he moved back to Michigan and began a career in real estate.

He met Jennie Stevens and married her. Just two short years into their marriage, Jennie Lake was diagnosed with tuberculosis and heart disease. Over the next couple of years, the condition worsened and the doctors resigned to the fact that it was only a matter of time before she would die. John allowed this situation to provoke him into faith, after being exposed to such death and disease from a young age he had a hatred for such things. When he would read the word of God he saw that his Christian experience was less than the promised "power of the Holy Spirit".

As Jennie was on her death bed and perhaps taking her final breaths, Lake was overcome with anger over sickness and threw his bible against the fireplace mantle! When he went to pick up his bible it was opened to Acts chapter 10:38 which says: "God anointed Jesus of Nazareth with the Holy Ghost and with power: who went about doing good, and healing all that were oppressed of the devil; for God was with him." Lake had a surge of faith in that moment and sent a telegram to Dowie asking him to pray. Within an hour of Dowie's prayer, she was fully healed! Not long after

Jennie was healed, God began to speak to Lake about going into full time ministry. After some time of contemplation and seeking the Lord, God confirmed to John and Jennie separately that they were to move to South Africa to begin their life of ministry.

It was in April 1907 when he closed his office door for the last time and disposed of his bank account by giving to various religious and educational institutions. Lake then started out in independent evangelistic work with a single dollar, being absolutely dependent upon the Lord, along the faith lines of George Muller of England and Hudson Taylor of the 'China Inland Mission'. John and Jennie gave away all that they had, John forsook his mega-salary and they went on their way alongside some of their friends as ministry partners.

Ministry in South Africa when they arrived in South Africa, they had no money. The problem was that they needed at least $125 in order to clear customs. They nervously waited for their turn in line, rehearsing what they would say to the immigration officer. They were in desperate need of a miracle, as the law read that they would be subject to deportation as quickly as they arrived in South Africa.

"God would supply his every need" (PHILIPPIANS 4:19). Just as they were about to get to the front of the line, John felt a tap on his shoulder… A man was standing behind John and said "excuse me sir, can I have a word with you?" John nervously steps out of line at the man's request and the man said "when I saw you and your family in line, the Lord told me to give you $200 cash". The Lord provided just enough money for John and his family to enter the country.

But their needs didn't stop there. The Lakes and their crew had no ministry contact in Johannesburg. Soon after they cleared customs, a woman approached John's friends and asked how many people are in their family, when they told her, she responded "no, not you" and went over to John and asked the same question. John replied "9" and she said "you're the ones!" She went on to tell John that the Lord had spoken to her last night that she was to give her home to a family of 9 people who are coming from America to do God's work.

John, Jennie and their crew rejoiced in the dramatic provision of the Lord. Their time in South Africa was marked with waves of revival, there were multitudes saved, healed and delivered over the course of their 5 year ministry tour in South Africa. Over a five year period in South Africa Lake saw 1,000,000 converts, planted hundreds of churches, and raised up over

1000 local ministers.

Shortly after the Lake family and their team arrived in South Africa an event took place. A mighty plague broke out and swept across the nation; the death count was climbing dramatically. So much so that there was a surplus of corpses who were victims of the plague and there was no one to bury the dead; if someone was to come in contact with a dead body they would most certainly become infected and their death sentence would immediately begin.

John G. Lake shocked the medical officials because he, without any gloves or protective clothing began burying the dead. Physicians in a panic approached John and rebuked him for coming in contact with the dead, John boldly responded "when the disease comes in contact with my skin, you can watch it die". The doctors thought he was insane, so he challenged them to put a drop of the plague on his skin and watch it under a microscope. When they did so, John was right! The plague cells literally burned up the second they came in contact with his skin!

Over an approximately five year period, over 100,000 healings were reported. Lake's church was never large yet thousands came from all over the country and the world to receive prayer. In 1920, he felt called to move to Portland, Oregon and start a healing room ministry there.

Similar healings were reported during these years as well. He ministered in churches in California, then returned to pastor in Portland for a season, and finally settled back in Spokane for the remainder of his life. Lake continued his ministry in North America until his death in 1935, and like Smith Wigglesworth, he fought an outstanding fight and ran a great race, right to the very end.

Lord, we heard how You used John Knox, Apostle Joseph Ayo Babalola, John G. Lake, and the early men and women. How we wish there were another Knox, Lake and Babalola now that could help us! Gideon in Judges 6: 12-14 asked a question that anyone in this present age that longed to be used of God should ask. *"And the angel of the Lord appeared unto, and said unto him, The LORD is with thee, thou mighty man of valour. And Gideon said unto him, Oh my Lord, if the LORD be with us, why then is all this befallen us? <u>AND WHERE BE ALL HIS MIRACLES WHICH OUR FATHERS TOLD US OF</u>, saying, Did not the LORD bring us up from Egypt? But now the LORD hath* *forsaken us, and delivered us into the hands of the Midianites"*

History is bound to repeat itself in greater dimensions in this generation of ours if only we are ready! You are the one we are waiting for! You are the John the Baptist of our time. You are the Lake, Moses, Apostle Paul, Knox, Babalola, et cetera of our time. Are you are ready?

THE WOMAN KATHRYN KUHLMAN
I BELIEVE IN MIRACLE

What God started with the early men did not stop with them! During the life of Jesus on earth, the first words He used when He was recruiting His men for service were: "follow Me" **Matthew 4:19**. When they followed Him and were now beginning to fellowship with Him, He introduced three new words to them that would determine the ultimate dimension of intimacy and true spiritual union they would have with Him.

Words which when obeyed would determine depths of joy unspeakable in their hearts; guarantee laudable accomplishments in their lives and ministries; peace in their hearts and cause them to experience the full benefits of the salvation prepared for them and so much more. These three words were: **"Abide in Me."John 15:4**.

Oh! How many of us in the church today still treasure these words-Abide in Me? This is the reason many faint amongst us. Not taking heed to these words has robbed many of us of the power, miracles and signs Jesus promised. When we follow and abide in Him, then we can share in His life. When we follow and abide in Him then we will be productive as He is.

I want to share the story of a woman who desired nothing else but to abide with Her Master and Friend-the Holy Spirit. A vessel that carried the presence of God tangibly; a woman who believes and saw miracles wrought in her ministry.

To start with, let me say what Pastor Benny Hinn shared about his experience with this great vessel in God's Hand:

"In 1973, Four days before Christmas I went with a friend of mine, Jim Poynter, on a charter bus trip from Toronto to Pittsburgh to a meeting of Kathryn Kuhlman. It would be a day that would change my life forever! I knew very little about her ministry, but when we arrived at the First Presbyterian Church in downtown Pittsburgh, hundreds of people were already there, though the doors wouldn't

open for several hours. As I stood in line, I suddenly began to shake. Nothing like that had ever happened before. It didn't stop. I was too embarrassed to tell Jim or anyone around me. Even when we got to our seats on the third row of the auditorium, the shaking continued. The longer it continued, the more beautiful it became. Then Kathryn Kuhlman appeared on stage.

The atmosphere in the building changed immediately. Everyone began singing "How Great Thou Art." Tears gushed down my face. It was a feeling of intense glory. I was literally singing the words from my soul. In my young Christian experience, God had touched me before, but never as He was touching me that day. It was as if the waves of a gentle breeze were flowing around me. As the evangelist began ministering to the people, I was so lost in the Spirit that all I could whisper was, "Dear Jesus, please have mercy on me." I felt so unworthy. Again and again, I said the words. The three-hour service may have seemed long to some, but to me it seemed like a fleeting moment. I saw the deaf begin to hear; I saw people rise from their wheelchairs, saw tumours vanish, and so much more. Then everything stopped. I prayed silently, "Please, Lord, don't ever let this meeting end."

Kathryn was burying her head in her hands, sobbing so loudly that everything came to a standstill. Then, standing just a few feet in front of me, her eyes seemed aflame as she took on a boldness I had never seen in anyone before. She began pleading as she looked out over the audience, "Please, don't grieve the Holy Spirit!"

Forty years after, I can still see her eyes. It was as if they were looking straight at me. Then she said, "Don't you understand? He's all I've got!" I thought, "What is she talking about?" She continued speaking, "Please! Don't wound Him. He's all I've got. Don't wound the One I love!"

I will never forget those words. I can remember the intensity of her breathing when she said them. Those moments are etched permanently into my memory. Then she pointed her finger down at me and said with such powerful clarity, "He's more real than anything in the world!" At that moment, I cried and said, "I've got to have this!" Then, within moments, the service was over. I was shaken to the core. God had used that service and His mighty evangelist to reveal His power that day.

All the way back to Toronto, I kept thinking, "What did she mean? What was she saying when she talked about the Holy Spirit?" I was totally exhausted when I arrived home, but I could not sleep. As I lay on my bed, I felt as if someone were pulling me off the mattress and onto my knees. It was a strange sensation, but I didn't resist. I had never spoken to the Holy Spirit before. I didn't know He could be addressed that way.

Finally, I prayed, "Holy Spirit, Kathryn Kuhlman says You are her Friend. I don't think I know You. Before today, I thought I did. But after that meeting, I realize I really don't. I don't think I know You." Then, like a child with my hands raised, I asked, "Can I meet You? Can I really meet You?" A few brief moments passed, then like a jolt of electricity my body began to vibrate all over again, exactly like at the church in Pittsburgh. I was afraid to open my eyes. I felt like a warm blanket of God's power was wrapped all over me. That continued until I finally dropped off to sleep that night. Even then, I still didn't realize all that had happened to me. The next morning, three days before Christmas, I awoke and the first words I spoke to my newfound Friend were, "Good morning, Holy Spirit!" At that instant, I knew He was there with me. As I opened my Bible, He was there sitting beside me. From that moment, everything about the Bible, my prayer life, my worship, and my relationship with God took on an entirely new dimension. For the next eight hours I had an incredible experience with the Holy Spirit that changed the course. Tears of wonderment and joy coursed down my cheeks. I had just turned twenty-one. Christmas was just around the corner. I had received the best present ever! Less than a year later, God would open the door for me to step behind a pulpit to preach for the first time, and in that moment He would simultaneously heal a lifelong stuttering problem and give birth to a ministry that would eventually reach around the globe."

The ministry of Kathryn Kuhlman laid a foundation for the workings of the Holy Spirit in the lives of countless thousands throughout the world. Her unique ministry shifted the focus of the body of Christ from the outward show of the supernatural gifts of the Holy Spirit back to the Giver of the Gifts the Holy Spirit. Miss Kathryn was an example of one who fearlessly paid the price to walk in the service of God.

Kathryn Johanna Kuhlman was born on May 9, 1907, in Concordia, Missouri to German-American parents, Joseph Adolph and Emma Kuhlman. She was one of four children. Kathryn became born-again at the age of fourteen in the Methodist Church of Concordia, Missouri. In her own words, she said of that experience and her ministry: "It was the beginning of something that changed my whole life. All that I knew was the glorious new birth experience, and (as a young girl) when I went to preach to those farmers in Idaho, I could tell them nothing more than what I had experienced: that Jesus would forgive their sins. So, I preached salvation all across Idaho to every farmer, to everyone who would listen; but gradually I began to realize there was someone besides the Father and the Son – there was this Third Person of the Trinity. I felt compelled to know more regarding Him and, as I began searching and studying God's Word, I could see that divine healing also was in the atonement."

One day, in Pennsylvania in the old Billy Sunday Tabernacle. She went to preach in Franklin in 1946, and it was in the third service, as she was preaching on the Holy Spirit, sharing with God's precious people the little according to her she knew about that Third Person of the Trinity. She mentioned about people in the service getting healed. The next night, before she began to preach, a woman stood up and said, 'Pardon me Miss Kuhlman, but I have a testimony to give. While you were preaching last night I had a strange sensation in my body, and I knew I had been healed. I knew it. Today I went to my doctor, and he confirmed that I was.' the woman was healed of a tumour. And that was the beginning and the first of miracle that took place in her ministry. This happened without the laying on of hands, without any special prayer; it just happened as she was preaching on the power of the Holy Spirit. Since that time, there have been thousands and thousands of healings. WHAT IS THE SECRET? It is the Third Person of the Trinity – the Holy Spirit!"

In 1948 Kuhlman held a series of meetings at Carnegie Hall in Pittsburgh. She eventually moved to Pittsburgh in 1950, and continued to hold meetings at Carnegie Hall until 1971. She was used by God to bring the charismatic message to many denominational churches, including the Catholic Church. (She received a lot of criticism over this and was accused of being a closet Catholic.) These were her best known years. Her style was flamboyant. She would hold her famous miracle services and the auditorium were filled to capacity every time. Hundreds of people were healed in her meetings, and even while listening to her on the radio or television. People she prayed for would often be hit with the power of God and be "slain in the Spirit." Kuhlman never claimed that she was the healer. She always pointed people to Jesus as their healer.

Kuhlman's methodology is simply by honouring the Holy Spirit and by being in God's presence. In one thrilling testimonial, Kathryn writes in

Nothing Is Impossible with God that a woman who was afflicted with cancer shared the following: "Miss Kuhlman was walking back and forth across the stage. She wasn't screaming or yelling, as I had thought she would be. She wasn't even preaching, just talking. She said, 'I don't want anyone to come up here on the stage until you have been healed.' Amazing, I thought to myself. I had pictured her slapping people on the forehead, vibrating and shaking, screaming commands for the Lord to heal some poor wretch. It wasn't that way, but people started coming forward, testifying that they had been healed while they were sitting in their seats."

In the midst of the high-spirited testimonies and worship, something amazing transpired. She writes: "Something else happened. I discovered I couldn't move my arms or legs. More surprising still, it didn't bother me to sit there paralyzed. In fact, it was altogether a very wonderful feeling. Mom later told me that Miss Kuhlman said someone was being healed of cancer, but I didn't hear it. As a matter of fact, I didn't hear much of anything during this time. When the wonderful feeling passed, a new feeling, a conviction, took its place—a deep conviction that I no longer had cancer."

A short time later, she went to the doctor, and he told her that the biopsy was entirely negative. They found no malignancy whatsoever. She writes that she questioned the doctor, saying, "I thought the first biopsy showed total malignancy." He shrugged. "It did, but when you got in there, everything was fine. I don't think you are going to have any trouble at all.'"

There were remarkable accounts like this transpiring every time that Kuhlman held a crusade. Individuals were getting out wheelchairs, and lives were being restored.

Roberts Liardon writes:
"On one occasion, a five-year-old boy, crippled from birth, walked to Kathryn's platform without assistance. On another, a woman, who had been crippled and confined to a wheelchair for twelve years walked to the platform without aid from her husband. A man from Philadelphia, who had received a pacemaker eight months earlier, felt intense pain in his chest after Kathryn laid hands upon him. Returning home, he found the scar gone from his chest where the pacemaker had been implanted, and he couldn't tell if the pacemaker was functioning. Later, when the doctor took x-rays, he discovered the pacemaker was gone, and the man's heart healed. **It was common for tumours to dissolve, cancers to fall off, the blind to see and the deaf to hear. Migraine headaches were healed instantly. Even teeth were divinely filled.** It would be impossible to list the miracles that the ministry of Kathryn Kuhlman witnessed! God alone knows."

Kathryn Kuhlman arguably became the most influential figure of the charismatic renewal, transforming a whole generation's understanding of healing and crusade evangelism. She showed an entire generation how to love and have fellowship with the Holy Spirit. She revealed the Holy Spirit as a friend and His purpose was to point us to Jesus. She dedicated her entire life to One whom she have never seen. Kathryn walked in the authority of what the Church should be like, a forerunner of the true "Bride of Christ."

We are at the moment where more than ever, in the history of man, God is willing and looking for willing hearts to demonstrate His power in order to dismantle satanic activities and influences on mankind. Gifts of the Spirit are not for the hierarchy of the church nor does it has gender dichotomy. Any one of us whether man, woman, boy, girl, lowborn, highborn, educated or un-educated can demonstrate God to this generation.

THE MAN BENSON IDAHOSA
If I Be A Man of God...

"As a young Christian, I once heard my pastor say during a morning service that Christians could raise the dead in the name of the Lord Jesus Christ. I believed it with all my heart. And flying around on my bicycle in those days, I went through the city of Benin in search of a dead person to raise to life. After about five hours of hard searching I found a compound where a little girl had died a few hours before. The corpse had been cleaned and prepared for burial. I walked boldly up to the father of the dead child. "The God whom I serve can bring your baby back to life," I told him. "Will you permit me to pray for the child and bring her back to life?" The man was startled, but he agreed. With great enthusiasm, I walked into the room and up to the bed. The child was cold and dead. With strong faith in the Lord, I called on the Lord to restore the child back to life. I turned to the corpse and called it by name, "Arise in the name of the Lord Jesus Christ." Oh Glory to God! The corpse sneezed, heavily, alas. The child had come back to life!" Benson Idahosa

Since the beginning of creation God has always raised up people to bring revival to their generation. In every generation God always find for Himself a man He lavishes His anointing and glory on. A question often posed is, can we do what the early men did? Can God do with us what He did with our fathers? The answer is yes of course! **And these signs will follow those who believe in my name they will cast out demons they will speak in other tongues and... will heal the sick." Luke 8:50.** Believe is the door that opens up the supernatural. God wants us to believe like the saints of old. He wants to release miracles like we see from the beginning to the end of the Bible.

We are living in an exciting time! It's the last days- the only days that each of us has the privilege to house the glory of the Lord. The Father wants to endorse our ministries with supernatural occurrences. He wants to do miracles, raise the dead, heal the sick and do wonders through you and I. We were created to see them happen; we were created to be them. God want AIDS sufferers healed, blind see, the lame walk, the dead raised, the gospel preached to the poor!

Bishop Benson Andrew Idahosa was born on September 11, 1938. He was a Charismatic Pentecostal preacher, and the founder of the Church of God Mission International. Papa Idahosa was born in Benin (now Edo state) as an unhealthy child into a poor family. His health was so bad that his father instructed the Mother to throw him away. The mother did throw him away, but after a while she took him back. This caused a temporary separation between his parents. Young Idahosa constantly had fainting spells as a child, and on one of his spells his mother abandoned him at a rubbish heap presuming him dead. Hours later, the mother came back and rescued him. He grew up in a poor household. Like most of the surrounding houses, his family home was a mud house. This reality denied him access to education until he was fourteen years old, when he was able to attend a local government school. He was so poor that he could not afford a pair of shoes until he was eighteen years old.

In 1952, through a dramatic incident Idahosa became a Christian in an Assemblies of God Church in Benin. His conversion was dramatic and his calling supernatural. He was converted by Pastor Okpo on a football field one Sunday afternoon while playing soccer with his teammates. Thus, young Benson became the first Bini member of Pastor Okpo's small congregation.

After his conversion he read the whole of John's Gospel and decided he had to witness to his friends. This was the beginning of Idahosa's preaching the Gospel. He later sought after the experience of Baptism in the Spirit and he asked the Pastor at the Assemblies of God to pray for him. He was filled with the Spirit and spoke in tongues. After this experience Idahosa began to preach in the different villages organizing open air meetings. He did this in the evening while he worked for a shoe company during the day. He was also an active and committed member of the Assemblies of God Church where he was converted.

The open air meetings witnessed people being healed of epilepsy and many other sicknesses. Other miracles were also happening in these meetings. The news about the open air meetings started to spread to other villages and this led to more evangelistic activities. In order to reach more people with the Gospel he bought a motorcycle to help him travel to distant villages to conduct Gospel meetings. In June 1967, Idahosa lost his father during the Civil War riots.

A year later, during one night, his room was filled with God's presence and he was awoken from sleep by a voice. It was the Lord speaking to him about his future mission; "I have called you that you might take the gospel around the world in my name, preach the gospel, and I will confirm my word with signs following. After this experience he began to do more evangelistic meetings and outreaches. He would ask the Chiefs who head the villages for permission to conduct an evangelistic meeting in their village. They responded and more people were saved through his ministry. He directed the converts to existing Pentecostal Churches such as the Assemblies of God. Due to his evangelistic activities Idahosa soon became a leader under Pastor Okpo (the pastor at the Assemblies of God Church where he became a Christian) who gave him directions in ministry. However this did not last long as Idahosa decided to follow his own vision and establish a Church.

By 1971, he had established churches all over Nigeria and Ghana. Known for his boldness, power and prosperity-based preaching, as well as an enormous faith in the supernatural, he was instrumental to the strong wave of revival in Christianity that occurred between the 1970s and 1990s in Nigeria. He is regarded by Christian's foes as the father of Pentecostalism in Nigeria, and was the founding President of the Pentecostal Fellowship of Nigeria (PFN). Many prominent Nigerian pastors like Ayo Oritsejafor , David Oyedepo, Johnson Suleman, David Ogbueli, Felix Omobude, Fred Addo and Chris Oyakhilome were his protégés.

"I know of no young black in all of Africa who is reaching millions as Benson is, in crusades with hundreds of thousands in attendance, in his weekly nationwide telecast, in his Bible School, training eager students from several nations. He also conducts campaigns in Sweden, Singapore, Malaysia, Korea, Australia and the United States, where he often appeared on national religious telecasts. His burden for souls, his ministry of healing and miracles, even to the raising of several dead, demonstrates he is especially called of the Lord in these end times." Mrs. **Gordon Freda Lindsay**

Benson Idahosa is sought after by everyone in his state, from government officials to beggars. When they posed questions and explained their problems to this man they received instantaneous miracle solutions, just as people did in Bible days with God's prophets. And the people get miraculous answers from this mighty leader of God's people. Dr. Ben Akosa

The Secret of His Success

Bishop Idahosa operated in faith and he had a robust faith. He believed and trusted God with a childlike faith. He once said that living a daily life of absolute faith in God is the only secret to great success. He believed God for everything. "All things are possible to him that believes." He spent quality time in prayer and in the study of God's Word.

People talk about leaving their footprints in the sands of time; I think sand will be washed away by floods. Bishop Idahosa has left an enduring legacy in the hearts of men; in the Christian landscape of Nigeria and beyond, and ultimately in heaven. Where are you leaving your prints?

THE MAN SMITH WIGGLESWORTH
Apostle of Faith

Smith Wigglesworth was without doubt one of the most anointed men of God that has lived in recent times. He was known as the Apostle of Faith, and if anyone deserved to be described as "full of faith and of the Holy Ghost", it was him. He lived and walked continually in the presence of God. And the miracles that accompanied his ministry were of the sort that has seldom been seen since the days of the apostles. People born blind and deaf, cripples-twisted and deformed by disease, others on death's door with cancer or sickness of every kind, - all were healed by the mighty power of God. Even the dead were raised.

Throughout scripture we see God using ordinary people for the sake of His mission. Our Lord did not call the popular, rich or successful to further His ministry, but rather, the poor, broken and faithful. I can only imagine how confused the Pharisees and religious leaders must have been while looking at the team of people that proclaimed the gospel.

If you ever feel like you are not worthy enough, remember that Jesus used a bunch of ordinary men and women to share Hope to a hopeless and near dead world. In Him, we find renewal and power. Jesus didn't call the equipped, He equipped the called. And no matter how ordinary you may appear today even right now even as you are holding this book, the same power that conquered the grave, wrought great wonders with the early men lives or can live within you!

Culture and the world put a lot of stock in credentials. If men want to hire you for a job, they want to know are you capable of doing the work? If they want to ask someone for advice, they want to know if they are familiar with the subject matter or the job. To men, the more titles, Bsc., diplomas, and achievements a person has to their name, the more qualified they are. Generally, this is a prudent attitude for approaching the world, but God has a way of turning our preconceptions upside-down, especially when it comes to a man He wants to use.

Smith Wigglesworth was born in 1859 to a very poor family. His father did manual labour, for very little pay. Smith himself went to work at the age of six to help with the family income. At six he was pulling turnips and at seven he was working in a woollen mill twelve hours a day. His parents did not know God, but Smith hungered in his heart to know Him. Even as a youngster he would pray in the fields. His grandmother was the critical Christian in his life.

She was a Wesleyan Methodist and would take Smith to meetings with her. At one of these meetings there was a song being sung about Jesus as the lamb and Smith came into the realization of God's love for him and his decision to believe Christ for his salvation was decided that day.

This conversion happened at Methodists when he was eight years of age. He was immediately filled with the desire to evangelize and led his own mother to Christ. His was hungry for God and hungry for souls. He was in the choir of the local Episcopal Church. "When most of the boys in the choir were twelve years of age they had to be confirmed by the bishop. I was not twelve, but between nine and ten, when the bishop laid his hands on me. I can remember that as he imposed his hands I had a similar experience to the one I had forty years later when I was baptized in the Holy Spirit. My whole body was filled with the consciousness of God's presence, a consciousness that remained with me for days. After the confirmation service all the other boys were swearing and quarrelling and I wondered what had made the difference between them and me."

Smith has various church experiences as he was growing up. He first went to an Episcopal church and then at thirteen a Wesleyan Methodist church. When he was sixteen he became involved in the Salvation Army. He felt deeply called to fast and pray for lost souls. He saw many people come to

Christ. At seventeen a mentor shared with him about water baptism and he decided to be baptized. The Salvation Army was experiencing a tremendous level of the power of God in those days. He describes meetings where "many would be prostrated under the power of the Spirit, sometimes for as long as twenty-four hours at a time." They would pray and fast and cry out for the salvation of fifty or a hundred people for the week and they would see what they had prayed for.

At eighteen, Smith left the factory and became a plumber. He moved to Liverpool when he was twenty and continued to work during the day and minister during his free time. He felt called to minister to young people and brought them to meetings. These were destitute and ragged children, whom he would often feed and care for. Hundreds were saved. Smith was often asked to speak in Salvation meetings and he would break down and weep under the power of God. Many would come to repentance in those meetings through this untrained man. At twenty-three he returned back Bradford and continued his work with the Salvation Army.

In Bradford, Smith met Mary Jane Featherstone, known as Polly, the daughter of a temperance lecturer. She left home and went to Bradford to take a servants job. One night she was drawn to a Salvation Army meeting. She listened to the woman evangelist, Gipsy Tillie Smith, and gave her heart to Christ. Smith was in that meeting and saw her heart for God. Polly became an enthusiastic Salvationist and was granted a commission by General Booth. They developed a friendship, but Polly went to Scotland to help with a new Salvationist work. She eventually moved back to Bradford and married Smith, who was very much in love with her.

The couple worked together to evangelize the lost. They opened a small church in a poor part of town. Polly would preach and Smith would make the altar calls. For a season, however, Smith became so busy with his plumbing work that his evangelistic fervour began to wane. Polly continued on, bringing Smith to conviction. One day while Smith was working in the town of Leeds he heard of a divine healing meeting. He shared with Polly about it. She needed healing and so they went to a meeting, and Polly was healed.

Smith struggled with the reality of healing, while being ill himself. He decided to give up the medicine that he was taking and trust God. He was healed. They had five children, a girl and four boys. One morning two of the boys were sick. The power of God came and they prayed for the boys and they were instantly healed. Smith struggled with the idea that God would use him to heal the sick in general. He would gather up a group of people and drive them to get prayer in Leeds. The leaders of the meeting were going to a convention and left Smith in charge. He was horrified. How could he lead a meeting about divine healing? He tried to pass it off to someone else but could not. Finally he led the meeting and several people were healed. That was it. From then on Smith began to pray for people for healing.

Smith had another leap to make. He had heard about the Pentecostals who were being baptized in the Holy Spirit. He went to meetings and was so hungry for God he created a disturbance and church members asked him to stop. He went to prayer and prayed for four days. Finally he was getting ready to head home and the vicar's wife prayed for him and he fell under the power of God and spoke in tongues. Everything changed after that. He would walk by people and they would come under the conviction of the Holy Spirit and be saved. He began to see miracles and healings and the glory of God would fall when he prayed and preached.

Smith had to respond to the many calls that came in and gave up his business for the ministry. Polly unexpectedly died in 1913, and this was a real blow to Smith. He prayed for her and commanded that death release her. She did arise but said to "Smith - the Lord wants me." His heartbroken response was "If the Lord wants you, I will not hold you". She had been his light and joy for all the years of their marriage, and he grieved deeply over the loss. After his wife was buried, he went to her grave, feeling like he wanted to die. When God told him to get up and go Smith told him only if you "give to me a double portion of the Spirit – my wife's and my own – I would go and preach the Gospel. God was gracious to me and answered my request." His daughter Alice and son-in-law James Salter began to travel with him to handle his affairs.

Smith would pray and the blind would see, and the deaf were healed, people came out of wheelchairs, and cancers were destroyed. One remarkable story is when He prayed for a woman in a hospital. While he and a friend were praying she died. He took her out of the bed stood her against the wall and said "in the name of Jesus I rebuke this death". Her whole body began to tremble. Then he said "in the name of Jesus walk", and she walked. Everywhere he would go he would teach and then show the power of God. He began to receive requests from all over the world. He taught in Europe, Asia, New Zealand and many other areas. When the crowds became very large he began a "wholesale healing". He would have everyone who needed healing lay hands on themselves and then he would pray. Hundreds would be healed at one time.

Over Smith's ministry it was confirmed that thousands were saved and healed and he impacted whole continents for Christ. Smith died on March 12, 1947 at the funeral, his dear friend Richardson said His ministry was based on four principles "First, read the Word of God. Second, consume the Word of God until it consumes you. Third believe the Word of God. Fourth, act on the Word."

A number of people were also raised literally from the dead under Smith's ministry. It has been recorded that Smith Wigglesworth raised 23 people from the dead in total, over the years of his ministry.

Wigglesworth's services never bored his audiences. At a meeting in Washington, D.C., a young girl on crutches entered the auditorium with the help of two other people. With no muscular ability, her legs dangled with her feet hanging vertically. When he invited those who wanted prayer to walk to the front, she struggled to go forward. Calling out to her, he said, "Stay right where you are. You are going to be a different girl when you leave this place." Inquiring about her condition, he learned she had never walked before. "This girl has no muscles in her legs; she has never walked before." He laid his hands on her head and prayed and cried, "In the name of Jesus Christ, walk!" Looking at her, he said, "You are afraid, aren't you?" "Yes," she replied. "There is no need to be. You are healed!" he shouted. "Walk! Walk!!" And praise God she did – like a baby just learning! Twice she walked, in that characteristic way, the length of the platform! Glory to God! When we left the room, her crutches were lying on the seat, and on reaching the sidewalk we saw her standing, as others do, talking with two girl friends." December 1934, Redemption Tidings: Washington, D.C

When Smith prays for the sick he gets right down to business. He rips off his coat and rolls up his sleeves. Lifting his hand to heaven he cries. "Are you ready?" If assent is given, he "lays hands upon the sick" and prays: then, with a cyclonic movement of the hands over the afflicted part or a resounding slap that can be distinctly heard) throughout the auditorium, he declares that they are "free," and commands them to stoop and bend over or to run up and down the aisle, as the case may be. His methods are spectacular, strenuous, and often humorous, but the results seem to justify the means, for at the close of the service when he asks all those who have been healed to stand, literally hundreds leap to their feet.

He was a man who walked and lived in the very presence of God. And yet, in many ways he was a very natural, down-to-earth man. And neither was he afraid of issuing the odd stern rebuke. His object was to be in constant, unbroken communion with the Father. He had spent hours and days fervently seeking God in his early years, but later, "Although his life was a combination of incessant prayer and praise, and every word and work was an act of worship, he was not given to protracted periods of fasting and prayer." Instead, he had learned the secret of being in continuous, intimate communion with God (sometimes withdrawing quietly into himself for this purpose), even when he was in a crowd of people. He walked by faith, and he was "in the Spirit" at all times. This was one vital secret to his success. He said, "There are two sides to this Baptism: The first is, you possess the Spirit; the second is that the Spirit possesses you." He had counted the cost, and everything was God's. He was a man who truly understood GODLY AUTHORITY, and he WALKED in it by faith. He said, "'Be filled with the Spirit,' i.e., be CRAMMED with the Spirit, so filled that there will be no room left for anything else."

On one occasion, he recalled, "I was travelling to Cardiff in South Wales. I had been much in prayer on the journey. The carriage was full of people whom I knew to be unsaved, but as there was so much talking and joking I could not get in a word for my Master. As the train was nearing the station, I thought I would wash my hands and as I returned to the carriage, a man jumped up and said, 'Sir, you convince me of sin,' and fell on his knees there and then. Soon the whole carriages of people were crying out the same way. They said, 'Who are you? What are you? You convince us all of sin'"

There is power in the name of Jesus. Let us apprehend it, the power of His resurrection, the power of His compassion, the power of His love. Love will break the hardest thing – there is nothing it will not break.

NOTE
I believe that the coming apostolic ministries, who will be bearers of true Revival in these last days, will combine the daring, miracle-working faith of Smith Wigglesworth and other early men and women. What glorious days ahead of us! Smith Wigglesworth died in 1946 at the ripe old age of 87, a flame of God to the very end.

The greatest revival in the history of mankind is coming to Planet earth soon! God is about releasing mightier anointing. He is now looking for men and women whom He can entrust with such an anointing. God is looking for men and women who hunger and thirst after Him, who press forward into the deep things of God, and who will be willing to pay the price and spent much time alone with Him. Men Like Elisha, who would not let go of Elijah until he had received a double portion of that great prophet's anointing, they will never let go of God until He blesses them with a similar supernatural empowerment.

God is looking for men with humble hearts; men who will sacrifice everything for the cause of Christ and who will stand in the gap as servant-leaders for their families and for Christ's Church.

THE MAN STEPHEN
Ordinary Deacon. Full of Faith and of the Holy Spirit

When I used the word 'ordinary' I don't mean to demean, disgrace or degrade the office of deaconry or the person of Deacon Stephen. The use of word is only to convey that title or no title, theological qualification or not, clergy or laity is not a determining factor to a man that can carry the fire of God to his generation.

The Lord is looking for ordinary Christians through whom He can display His extraordinary nature. He wants to do mighty things through you and me. Some of us carry this negative mentality about us not being qualified for the Master's use; we need to break off this negative thinking. God doesn't want you to do what you can do by yourself; He wants to begin to do things through your life that only HE can do, where only He gets the glory. He wants to do mighty deeds that give witness to the reality of who He is in us. **Daniel 11:32 says, "But those who know their God will be strong and do great exploits."**

This generation will witness the rise of another great people God will do mighty acts through. What is a mighty act? Something that is bigger than what we can do in and of ourselves. I believe that we are a generation that will not drop the spiritual "baton," but we will hand the next generation a rich heritage of spiritual progress in the Lord so that they may run with an even greater level of glory and knowledge of Him than we've ever known before on earth.

Stephen was one of the outstanding characters in the early Church, and we read about him in Acts 6:5-15; 7:1-60; 8:2; 11:19; 22:20. He was a radiant, mighty soul-winner and the secret of his life and ministry is the fact that he was "a man full of the Holy Spirit" (Acts 6:5). It is important for us to understand that the Spirit-filled life is God's plan and provision for every Christian; the fullness of the Holy Spirit is not given to a spiritual aristocracy, to the more mature Christian, the minister or the missionary only. On the Day of Pentecost "all of them were filled with the Holy Spirit" (Acts 2:4); the promise is to "all" (Acts 2:39), and the command is to every Christian (Ephesians 5:18). As we look at Stephen we shall see what a man is like when he is full of the Holy Spirit.

In the days when the number of disciples began to be multiplied there developed a situation which caused the twelve to make a definite decision not to occupy themselves with serving tables, but to give themselves continually to prayer and to the ministry of the Word. How important it is for all God's ministers to be continually in prayer, and constantly feeding on the Scriptures of Truth. None of us can be strong in God unless we are diligently and constantly hearkening to what God has to say to you through His Word. You cannot know the power and the nature of God unless you partake of His inbreathed Word. Read it at morning and at night, and at every opportunity you get.

The Psalmist said that he had hid God's Word in his heart, that he might not sin against Him; and you will find that the more of God's Word you hide in your heart, the easier it is to live a holy life. As you receive with meekness the engrafted Word, you will find faith up springing within. And you will have life through the Word.

The twelve told the rest to look out for men to look after the business end of things. They were to be men of honest report and filled with the Holy Ghost. These were just ordinary men who were chosen, but they were filled with the Holy Spirit, and this infilling always lifts a man to a plane above the ordinary. It does not take a cultured or a learned man to fill a position in God's church; what God requires is a yielded, consecrated, holy life, and He can make of such a flame of fire. Baptized with the Holy Ghost and fire!

The multitude chose out seven men to serve tables. They were doubtless faithful in their appointed tasks, but we see that God soon had a better choice for two of them. Philip was so full of the Holy Ghost that he could have a revival wherever God put him down. Man chose him to serve tables, but God chose him to win souls. Oh! if I could only stir you up to see that as you are faithful in performing the humblest office, God can fill you with His Spirit and make you a chosen vessel for Himself, and promote you to a place of mighty ministry in the salvation of souls and in the healing of the sick. There is nothing impossible to a man filled with the Holy Ghost. It is beyond all human comprehension. When you are filled with the power of the Holy Ghost, God will wonderfully work wherever you go.

When you are filled with the Spirit you will know the voice of God. You have no conception what God can do through you when you are filled with His Spirit. Every day and every hour you can have the divine leading of God. To be filled with the Holy Ghost means much in every way. I have seen some who have been suffering for years, and when they have been filled with the Holy Ghost everything of their sickness has passed away. The Spirit of God has made real to them the life of Jesus and they have been completely liberated of every sickness and infirmity.

Look at Stephen, he was just an ordinary man chosen to serve tables. But the Holy Ghost was in him and he was full of faith and power, and did great wonders and miracles among the people. There was no resisting the wisdom and the spirit by which he spoke. How important it is that every man shall be filled with the Holy Spirit.

Tongues and Interpretation: "The divine will is that you should be filled with God; for the power of the Spirit to fill you with the mightiness of God. There is nothing God will withhold from a man filled with the Holy Ghost." I want to impress the importance of this upon you. It is not healing that I am presenting to you-it is the living Christ. It is a glorious fact that the Son of God came down to bring liberty to the captives.

How is it that the moment you are filled with the Holy Ghost persecution starts? It was so with the Lord Jesus Himself. We do not read of any persecutions before the Holy Spirit came down like a dove upon Him. Shortly after this we find that, after preaching in His home town, they wanted to throw Him over the brow of a hill. It was the same with the twelve disciples. They had no persecution before the day of Pentecost; but after they were filled with the Spirit, they were soon in prison. The devil and the priests of religion will always get stirred when a man is filled with the Spirit and does things in the power of the Spirit. And persecution is the greatest blessing to a church. When we have persecution we will have purity. If you desire to be filled with the Spirit you can count on one thing, and that is persecution. The Lord came to bring division, and even in your own household you may find three against two.

The Lord Jesus came to bring peace; and soon after you get peace within, you get persecution without. If you remain stationary, the devil and his agents will not disturb you much. But when you press on and go the whole length with God the enemy has you as a target. But God will vindicate you in the midst of the whole thing.

You people who are seeking the Baptism are entering a place where you will have persecution. Your best friends will leave you-or those you may esteem as your best friends. No good friend will ever leave you. But it is worthwhile. You enter into a realm of illumination, or revelation by the power of the Holy Ghost. He reveals the preciousness and the power of the blood of Christ. I find by the revelation of the Spirit that there is not one thing in me that the blood does not cleanse. I find that God sanctifies me by the blood and reveals that efficacy of the work by the Spirit.

Stephen was just an ordinary man clothed with the Divine. He was full of faith and power, and great wonders and miracles were wrought by him. Oh, this life in the Holy Ghost! this life of deep, inward revelation, of transformation from one state to another, of growing in grace and in all knowledge and in the power of the Spirit, the life and the mind of Christ being renewed in you, and of constant revelations of the might of His power. It is the only kind of thing that will enable us to stand. In this life, the Lord puts you in all sorts of places, and then reveals His power. If you will, all His power is at your disposal!

They were not able to resist the wisdom and spirit by which Stephen spoke, and so, full of rage, they brought him to the council. And God filled his face with a ray of heaven's light. It is worth being filled with the Spirit, no matter what it costs. Read the seventh chapter, the mighty prophetic utterance by this holy man. Without fear he tells them, "Ye stiff-necked and uncircumcised in heart, ye do always resist the Holy Ghost." And when they heard these things they were cut to the heart. There are two ways of being affected at the heart. Here they gnashed their teeth and cast him out of the city and stoned him. On the day of Pentecost, when they were pricked at the heart they cried out, "What shall we do?" They took the opposite way. The devil, if he can have his way, will cause you to commit murder. If Jesus has His way, you will repent.

And Stephen, full of the Holy Ghost, looked up steadfastly into heaven, and saw the glory of God, and the Son of man standing on the right hand of God. O, this being full of the Holy Ghost! How much it means. Stephen cried out, "Lord, lay not this sin to their charge." As he was full of the Spirit he was full of love, and he manifested the very same compassion for his enemies that Jesus did at Calvary. This being filled with the Holy Ghost means much in every way. It means constant filling, quickening, and a new life continually. Oh, it's lovely! We have a wonderful gospel and a great Saviour! If you will but be filled with the Holy Ghost you will have a constant spring within, yea, as your faith centres in the Lord Jesus, from within you shall flow rivers of living water.

The Greek words for "BE FILLED with the Holy Spirit" (Eph 5:18), should be translated, "BE BEING FILLED with the Holy Spirit". In other words, we are to be constantly seeking God so that we will become more and fuller of His Holy Spirit. Some people believe that we Christians only receive one infilling of God's Spirit in our lifetime. Such people may be sincere, but they are SINCERELY WRONG.

This book is about men and women of God who were not satisfied with an initial token of God's grace or presence in their lives. They were hungry for more, and in their desperation for greater and greater depths in God, they smashed through every barrier and overthrew every obstacle to experience an ever-greater measure of God's holy presence and glory, - and to gain an anointing the like of which has rarely been seen since the days of the apostles.

THE WOMAN AIMEE SEMPLE MCPHERSON
The Founder of Foursquare Gospel Church

Sister Aimee, twentieth-century evangelist was a woman ahead of her time. In an era when women were not allowed to vote, she refused to leave religion and other "important" pursuits to men. Sister Aimee Semple McPherson travelled across the United States and around the globe. She sparked revival, established a major evangelical centre in Los Angeles and changed the lives of countless individuals. She was one of the great heroines of the faith in American church history, a Pentecostal evangelist and founder of International Church of the Foursquare Gospel, the first interdenominational mega-church. Her dramatic, illustrated sermons throughout the 1920s and 30s opened the eyes of many people to the truths of the gospel. She became a great healing evangelist and media pioneer, being one of the first Christians to use radio to preach the gospel.

Women have played exciting roles as the drama of redemption and revival unfolds. "...I will pour out my Spirit upon all flesh..." has no separation for sexes. That one is a woman does not stop God from using her if she makes herself available for the Master's use. Women, your choices are limitless if only you can make yourself available. Every woman should seek God, what God did or will do with men He is also determined to do same with women. One thing I have learnt in life is, life is incomplete without women. We will consider the life of another woman that scored points for the kingdom of God. If you are a woman reading this book prepare for a mighty anointing coming on you to shake your world for Jesus Christ!

Aimee Kennedy was born on October 9, 1890 in a small town in Ontario to James Morgan and Minnie Kennedy, a Methodist and a Salvation Army devotee respectively, in Ontario, Canada. Her father, James Kennedy, was a struggling farmer. Her mother, Mildred "Minnie" Pearce was a member of the Salvation Army (1865; founded by William Booth [1829–1912] as a religious organization with military structure for the purpose of bettering life for the poor and evangelizing the world). Soon after Aimee's birth, her mother took her to the Salvation Army and dedicated her to God's service.

Aimee Semple McPherson is a name that is continually mentioned in sermons, magazines, newspapers and websites all over the world. I personally admire her and all of her efforts to bring forth the gospel of Jesus Christ to those who did not know him. Aimee and her mother are thought to be the first two women who travelled successfully across the United States in their automobile. Aimee introduced jazz music into the church. Her use of illustrated sermons and dramatization became very popular in her day and has carried on through the ages of time. We could say that she turned the religious world of her day upside down.

Sister Aimee was a gifted missionary and healing evangelist, editor, author and founder of the International Church of the Foursquare Gospel as said earlier that today has over 25,000 churches and over 3 million members. She became internationally famous as the leader of the 5,300-seat Angelus Temple in Echo Park, Los Angeles, where she conducted church in an attractive theatre-style. She often used extravagant props and effects that resembled Hollywood stage productions more than church services. The innovation worked well as great crowds flocked to her standing-room-only meetings, sometimes three times a day and seven days a week. She believed that the Gospel should be presented in an enjoyable and contemporary way and she saw thousands come to Christ through her ministry.

Although a church girl she began to slip into worldly activities during her teens but was invited by her father to attend Robert Semple's tent revival at Ingersoll, Ontario, Canada, during the winter months of 1907. She was not only converted to Christ during this time but also fell in love with this young Pentecostal preacher. A year later, she married Robert, He was 27 and she was 17 when they were married on August 28th 1908.

Two years after their marriage Robert and Aimee sailed to China. On their way, they stopped at Robert's parents who lived in Ireland. They took this little slot of time to rest, as Aimee was now pregnant. Their last stop on their way to China was in London. They stayed with a Christian millionaire named Cecil Polhill. The night before they were to leave for China from London, Cecil asked Aimee to "bring the message" to a crowd gathered at London's Albert Hall. Aimee reluctantly agreed to preach. This was something she had never done before. She was still a very young 19 year old woman who was absolutely terrified to stand before a crowd of 15,000. She had no clue what to do as she stood behind the platform. She opened her

Bible and it fell open to a particular Scripture that was illuminated to her by the Holy Spirit. She preached for almost one hour as the crowd was captivated by the power of the Holy Spirit. Needless to say, her first sermon was a success.

Aimee and Robert finally arrived in China in June of 1910. Robert immediately began to preach to the natives through an interpreter. The opportunities for preaching the Gospel were widespread in this area. One of their greatest problems in China was the sanitary conditions. Two months after the Semple's arrived; they were both hospitalized with malaria and dysentery. Five days after their second wedding anniversary, Robert died during the night in his hospital bed. One month after Robert's death, Aimee gave birth to a healthy baby girl. She named her daughter Roberta Star, in remembrance of her father. Aimee and her new baby returned to the United States to join Aimee's mother, now separated from her father and living in New York.

Aimee attended a Pentecostal camp meeting in Kitchener, Ontario during the summer of 1915. She found herself responding to the altar call at the end of one of the meetings. She came forward and was asked to raise her hands and pray aloud. She threw her arms into the air and began to pray for forgiveness. As she did this, the anointing of the Holy Spirit came upon her and she began to speak in tongues. She laughed and cried while her entire body shook under the power of God. As she reached out to touch others, they also began receiving the Holy Spirit. This was truly a day of new beginnings for Aimee Semple McPherson.

Aimee was a woman who did many peculiar things. Once at a Mission in Ontario, she had scheduled a meeting. No one showed up for the meeting, so Aimee took a chair and placed it on a curb next to a barber shop. She got on the chair, closed her eyes and raised her hands toward heaven to pray silently. She didn't move a muscle for a long period of time. A crowd soon began to gather around her wondering what this crazy woman was doing. After about an hour or so, she jumped off the chair onto the ground and said, "People, come and follow me, quick." The group of about 50 people followed her right into the mission where she was supposed to preach. By the end of the week, Amy was preaching to nightly crowds of 500.

Since the crowds were beginning to grow in number, Aimee decided to purchase a tent to hold her meetings in. She took this tent all over America preaching the Gospel of Jesus Christ. Aimee arrived back in New York City, where her mother, Minnie Kennedy, was working as a member of the

Salvation Army. Aimee cared for Roberta and worked at the Glad Tidings Mission. From Los Angeles in 1919, McPherson launched a series of meetings that catapulted her to national fame. Within a year, America's largest auditoriums could not hold the crowds. She goes along with too popular demand that she pray for the sick, and "stretcher days" became hallmarks of her campaigns.

Reporters marvelled at her oratorical skills: "Never did I hear such language from a human being. Without one moment's intermission, she would talk from an hour to an hour and a half, holding her audience spellbound." Pastors from many denominations threw their support behind her city-wide campaigns. In 1921 she decided to design and build Angelus Temple in Echo Park, Los Angeles. On January 1, 1923 the Temple was dedicated and Aimee committed herself to pasturing the growing flock. She held evangelistic tours, in such places as Australia, San Diego, San Francisco, Denver, Winnipeg, San Jose, and Canton, Ohio. And not only these, In addition she also wrote books, edited the Bridal Call and created a vibrant radio preaching ministry.

While she continued to preach "the four-square Gospel" (Jesus as the Only Saviour, the Great Physician, the Baptizer with the Holy Spirit, and the Coming Bridegroom), she become a citizen of note in a burgeoning city. Angelus Temple floats won prizes in Rose Bowl parades, and the Temple itself became a tourist attraction. The comings and goings of "Sister" (as she was affectionately known) from the city's Union Station drew more people than visits of presidents and other dignitaries.

Her public ministry at Angelus temple was extraordinary, resembling magnificent stage productions, drawing people who would never have thought to enter a church. Her illustrated sermons attracted the imagination of the lower classes as well as people from the middle and upper classes and those who worked in the entertainment industry. She employed a brass band, large choirs, costumes, and elaborate sets to draw people to church.

Her services became known for divine healing, where repentant would walk without crutches, regain lost eyesight, heal broken bones, and leave their wheelchairs to walk. Although her first manifestation of divine healing occurred in Corona, New York in 1917, it was not until she had the attention of major city newspapers, such as the Los Angeles Times and the New York Times that many people nationally learned of such phenomena occurring in her services. The critics had a field day but thousands flocked to her services. She never ceased to be loyal to the Pentecostal testimony and many were baptized in the Holy Spirit and spoke with tongues.

Aimee Semple McPherson impacted several of the Third Wave/Word-Faith preachers. She was Kathryn Kuhlman's spiritual mother. Benny Hinn revealed that he periodically visits Aimee McPherson's grave, where he says: "I felt a terrific anointing ... I was shaking all over ... trembling under the power of God ... `Dear God,' I said, `I feel the anointing.' ... I believe the anointing has lingered over Aimee's body."(Benny Hinn, April 7, 1991 sermon). Aimee made an amazing impact on her world as a preacher and founder of a vigorous evangelistic organisation. Her legacy lives on.

Tell me what would be you excuse for not shaking your world for the kingdom of God? We were all called to Change the World for God. Throughout the centuries, the men and women whom God has been able to use to rout the forces of darkness, to make a lasting impact upon the heathen for His Name and to establish a testimony for His glory, have always been few in number. God is looking today for men and women who will allow Him to use them to impact the world.

Let me drop this and do so with a sense of conviction: To someone reading this book, you are one of the agents we have been waiting for to bring the kingdom of God in this present generation. You are the one we have been waiting for!

THE MAN WILLIAM SEYMOUR
The Medium of Pentecost and the Champion of Azusa Street Revival

"What the Church needs today is not more machinery, not new organizations or methods, but MEN whom the Holy Spirit can use. The Holy Spirit does not flow through methods but through men. He does not come on machinery but on men. He does not anoint plans but men. Natural ability and educational advantages do not figure as factors in this matter; but capacity for faith, the ability to pray, the power of thorough consecration, the ability of self-littleness, and absolute losing of one's self in God's glory and an ever-present and insatiable yearning and seeking after all the fullness of God—men who can set the Church ablaze for God; not in a noisy showy way, but with an intense and quiet heat that melts and moves everything for God. God can work wonders if He can get suitable men". **E. M. Bounds**

William Joseph Seymour was born May 2, 1870 in Centerville, St. Mary's Parish, and Louisiana. His parents, Simon and Phyllis Seymour. Seymour was the oldest of ten children, but only three lived to adulthood. Information about Seymour's early years is generally sketchy. The family's religious affiliation appears to have been Catholic as the children were registered and baptized in the local Catholic church but was raised as a Baptist.

In 1890, Seymour left the rural South and moved north to Memphis, hoping to have a better life than what was found in the south. While there he worked as a porter and a truck driver. In 1893 he moved on to St. Louis and worked as a bartender. In 1895 Seymour moved yet further north to Indianapolis, Indiana, where he worked as a railroad porter and then waited on tables in a fashionable restaurant.

In Indianapolis he attended a revival at the Simpson Chapel Methodist Episcopal Church and was subsequently saved. There was something radical in Seymour's heart, however, and he left looking for a church which embraced a more supernatural and revelatory view of God. Seymour joined the "Evening Light Saints" for a short time. They were later to identify themselves as "The Church of God" headquartered in Anderson Indiana. The church embraced strict holiness standards, sanctification, and divine healing as a foundational doctrine. The "Saints" regularly saw people supernaturally healed and even a few raised from the dead. Seymour adopted their teachings and carried them forward as he developed his own ministry. They credentialed Seymour as a minister, but it appears he did not step into a full-time work.

In 1900 Seymour moved to Chicago, the centre of the Divine Healing Movement under John Alexander Dowie. Around 1901 Seymour moved on to Cincinnati, Ohio. It is suggested that, while in Cincinnati, Seymour attended "God's Bible School" started by Martin Wells Knapp. The school taught holiness, divine healing and pre-millennialism which directly aligned with Seymour's belief system. He was feeling a pull on his life to become a full-time minister of the gospel, but was reluctant to make the move. He succumbed to smallpox and was blinded in one eye. He believed that it was God's judgment for resisting the call into ministry.

Around 1902 Seymour left Cincinnati. In 1904 he was listed as a resident of Columbus, Ohio where he worked as a travelling salesman. He went on to Houston, Texas to be near family. He also began holding evangelistic meetings in Texas and Louisiana. By 1905 he felt that God had spoken to him clearly to go to Jackson, Mississippi to meet with a "significant coloured clergyman" who would give him more direction. It is believed to have been Charles Price Jones, a well-known Holiness preacher. Seymour remained there a short time and then returned to Houston. Once back in Houston Seymour took on a small congregation which had been started by a woman named Lucy Farrow. Farrow subsequently took a job, as a governess, with Charles F. Parham. Parham had been teaching on the Pentecostal baptism and speaking in tongues since 1900.

Parham opened the Houston Bible School in 1905, holding 10 week training sessions on Pentecostal theology. That theology included divine healing. Lucy Farrow encouraged Seymour to attend the school. Due to Jim Crow laws Seymour was not allowed to sit inside the classroom but had to sit in the hall and listen through the doorway. Seymour's Holiness theology expanded to include the Pentecostal experience. He worked with Parham as an evangelist in the African-American community for the next several months.

Then in February 1906 Seymour received an invitation to move to Los Angeles and take over a small Holiness Mission. He took the position and immediately began teaching on the Pentecostal experience. The doctrine was considered suspect by the Holiness community and Seymour was immediately rejected and locked out of the church. After Seymour was resistance just 2 days after arriving, he began preaching to his new congregation that speaking in tongue was the Bible evidence of the baptism in the Holy Spirit. Condemnation also came from the Holiness Church Association of Southern California with which the church had affiliation. Not everyone in the congregation, however, was troubled by Seymour's teaching.

Undaunted, Seymour, staying at the home of church member Edward S. Lee, accepted Lee's invitation to hold Bible studies and prayer meetings there. After this, he went to the home of Richard and Ruth Asbery at 214 North Bonnie Brae Street. Five weeks later, Lee became the first to speak in tongues. Seymour then shared Lee's testimony at a gathering on North Bonnie Brac and soon many began to speak in tongues. On April 9, 1906 the Spirit of God fell and several people began speaking in tongues. Once news of this phenomena got out the bible study began to grow very quickly.

The group moved to 312 Azusa Street and began a revival that would impact the world. The meetings in Azusa Street were dramatic. People "fell under the power", shook violently, jerked, and made loud noises. Fire was seen rising from the building to heaven and returning back down again. The "cloud of the Spirit" was so thick that children would play hide and seek in the midst of the meetings. Bands of angels were seen at the mission. Tongues given were often interpreted by visitors from other nations who recognized the language. Miracles and healings were common events. One man who had lost his arm in a machinery accident received a new one instantaneously. Seymour's cry was that God would receive the glory.

Word of these events travelled quickly in both the African-American and white communities. For several nights, speakers preached on the porch to the crowds on the street below. Believers from Hutchinson's mission, First New Testament Church, and various holiness congregations began to pray for the Pentecostal baptism. (Hutchinson herself was eventually baptized in the Spirit as was Seymour himself). The meetings at the Apostolic Faith Mission quickly caught the attention of the press due to the unusual nature of the worship. Between 300 and 350 people could get into the whitewashed 40 by 60 foot wood frame structure, with many others occasionally forced to stand outside. Church services were held on the first floor where the benches were placed in a rectangular pattern. Some of the benches were simply planks put on top of empty nail kegs. There was no elevated platform. There was no pulpit at the beginning of the revival.

The second floor housed the office of the mission and rooms for several residents including Seymour and his wife Jenny. It also had a large prayer room to handle the overflow from the altar services below. One seeker described it as follows: "Upstairs is a long room furnished with chairs and three California redwood planks, laid end to end on backless chairs. This is the Pentecostal upper room where sanctified souls seek Pentecostal fullness and go out speaking in new tongues."

Still, the revival advanced slowly during the summer months with only 150 people receiving "the gift of the Holy Ghost and the Bible evidence." But this changed in the fall as the revival gained momentum and people from far and wide began to attend. People even travelled all the way from North China to investigate the happenings after hearing that the promised latter rain was falling.

Stories of the revival spread quickly across North America to Europe and other parts of the world as participants travelled, testified, and published articles in sympathetic holiness publications.

Most who visited the mission came to receive the empowerment of Spirit baptism and be equipped with intelligible new languages for gospel preaching overseas. This would enable them to bypass the nuisance of formal language study. The Apostolic Faith reported: "God is solving the missionary problem, sending out new-tongued missionaries on the apostolic faith line, without purse or scrip, and the Lord is going before them preparing the way." Missionaries' home on furloughs also attended and spoke in tongues and in a few instances identified the languages being spoken. The recipients, however, usually depended on the Lord to identify the languages they had received.

African-Americans, Latinos, whites, and others prayed and sang together, creating a dimension of spiritual unity and equality, almost unprecedented for the time. It allowed men, women, and children to celebrate their unity in Christ and participate as led by the Spirit. Indeed, so unusual was the mixture of blacks and whites, that Bartleman enthusiastically exclaimed, "The colour line was washed away in the blood." He meant that in the sanctifying work of the Holy Spirit, the sin of racial prejudice had been removed by the cleansing blood of Jesus Christ.

Meanwhile, in late summer 1906, Charles Parham had begun leading another Pentecostal revival in Zion City, Illinois, among the followers of the nationally known faith healer John Alexander Dowie. Not until October did Parham leave for California, hoping to consolidate the faithful in Los Angeles within the wider network of Apostolic Faith believers, and second, to harness what he considered to be an unbridled religious enthusiasm.

On a worldwide scale, the Azusa Street revival contributed to a new Diaspora of missionaries who anticipated that global evangelization would be achieved by gospel preaching accompanied by miraculous signs and wonders (Acts 5:12). While only a small number of missionaries travelled from Azusa Street to minister overseas, it impacted many more that started other Pentecostal revival centres that surfaced as a result of hearing the news of the outpouring of the Spirit in Los Angeles. For many, the Azusa Street revival had inaugurated at long last the great end-times revival.

The unique interracial and intercultural dynamics at Azusa, however, accented both holiness of character and power to witness in an unusual demonstration of love and equality in the body of Christ. In this respect, it powerfully reminds us that the fullness of Pentecostal power will elude those who seek for power in their ministry above that of Christ like character.

On the Day of Pentecost, Jewish visitors from many countries stood bewildered as they heard the praises of God in their native languages (Acts 2:5–13). Some seriously asked, "What does this mean?" Others poked fun and failed to consider the significance of the occasion. Nonetheless, Peter, placing things in divine perspective, referred them to the words of Joel: "In the last days, God says, I will pour out my Spirit on all people" (Acts 2:17, NIV).

The Azusa Street revival illustrated the fundamental truth about the acquisition of spiritual power: The desire to love others and win the world for Christ begins with brokenness, repentance, and humility. "This move was the most powerful move of God on earth, which over the years resulted in 600 million people being swept into the Kingdom of God and gave birth to Pentecostal movement."Rev. Mosy Madugba. There will be a greater move of God in our time get ready!

God has given us much in these last days, and where much is given much will be required. God has no use for any man who is not hungering and thirsting for yet more of Himself and His righteousness. We need to wake up and be on the stretch to believe God. We have been seeing wonderful miracles and outpouring of His Spirit these last days and they are only a little of what we are going to see.

I believe that we are right on the threshold of wonderful things, but I want to emphasize that all these things will be through the power of the Holy Ghost.

God is raising up a new generation of spiritual warriors- new breed of revivalists; I believe you reading this book will be one of the emerging red-hot revivalists.

THE MAN ELIJAH
LET FIRE FALL...

The life of Elijah was unique and Holy Spirit-filled. Elijah's biography is an interesting storyline of a "wild, untutored child of the desert," who was given by God a high work and calling overwhelmed with great difficulties. The prophet Elijah is one of the most out of the ordinary and colourful people in the Bible, and God used him during an important time in Israel's history to oppose a wicked king and bring revival to the land. Elijah's ministry marked the beginning of the end of Baal worship in Israel.

There comes sometimes in the life of every Christian when he must find the spiritual strength and courage to stand alone and do the will of God. Elijah was such a man. The Bible calls him a Tishbite. We know nothing of his mother or of his father; in fact, we are not even sure where Tishba was. But God had prepared his heart and raised him up for this hour of need in the life of God's people. The name of Elijah and its meaning in Hebrew tells us much about a mother and father though they remain nameless. His name "Elijah" meant "my God is Jehovah." This rough-hewn man who has been called God's answer to Baal was one of the two men in scripture who had the privilege of being taken from this life without passing through death. Again and again God blessed this man who had courage to stand when all others knelt; to speak when all others held silence; to exercise his faith in the will of God when all others were faithless.

It was Elijah who stood with Jesus on the Mount of Transfiguration. Perhaps it was Elijah, one of the two men in white apparel who stood as Jesus ascended up into heaven and said, "Why stand ye, men of Galilee, gazing up into heaven. This same Jesus who is taken up will so come again in like manner.

Some Prophets are called prophets of words and others prophets of deeds. Elijah was certainly a prophet of deeds. In Elijah's spirit is the power that with¬held rain, parted rivers, healed the sick, and brought reformation to a backslidden people. Elijah, the man God appointed from the desert regions to go before kings, bringing the message of warning and repentance. Elijah was a human being just like any of us—a man of similar hopes and dreams, weaknesses and shortcomings, but also a man of deep faith in God. Elijah was a bold, direct-to-the-point prophet of God. By speaking the prophecies of God, he made fierce enemies, but his enemies could not overpower him.

The apostle James would later speak of Elijah's faith saying, "Elijah was a man with a nature like ours and he prayed earnestly that it would not rain; and it did not rain on the land for three years and six months. And he prayed again, and the heaven gave rain, and the earth produced its fruit" (James 5:17-18).

Like many of the prophets, Elijah did not seek to be God's messenger. Instead, God chose him for the job. Once called, Elijah did not hesitate to take on his mission, even though it appeared that his life would be threatened by the wicked king. Elijah set out at once for the capital city of Samaria to deliver the announcement to King Ahab. Then God sent Elijah into hiding as the drought dried up the streams and withered the crops of the nation (1 Kings 17:7-15; 1 Kings 18:1).

Withholding rain for three years and six months was the first miracle God did through Elijah. This brought severe famine throughout the kingdom. The purpose of this punishment was to bring the nation to repentance of its idolatry. Although unpleasant at the time, Elijah likely understood the potentially good effects of such punishment if Israel would repent of its sins. God always determines the magnitude and duration of punishment that He brings; and in this case, He moved Elijah to pray for an end of the rain and later for it to begin again.

The prophets of Baal were humiliated when they couldn't invoke their pagan god to end the drought and bring the needed rain upon the land. King Ahab and his officials were furious with Elijah, thinking that he was the cause of so much suffering in Israel; and they hunted for Elijah far into foreign lands (1 Kings 18:10). Elijah, the prophet was directed by God to appear before King Ahab again. "Then it happened, when Ahab saw Elijah that Ahab said to him 'Is that you, O troubler of Israel?' And he answered, 'I have not troubled Israel, but you and your father's house have, in that you have forsaken the commandments of the LORD and have followed the Baal's'" (1 Kings 18:17-19).

Elijah's greatest public miracle involved a contest with the 450 prophets of Baal and the 400 prophets of Asherah on Mount Carmel. Elijah invited these false prophets and all Israel to a demonstration to show that Baal had no power at all against the God of Israel. The outcome would demonstrate who served the true God (1 Kings 18:19-40). To show God's power, Elijah told the large crowd, "I alone am left a prophet of the LORD; but Baal's prophets are four hundred and fifty men" (1 Kings 18:22). Elijah continued, "How long will you falter between two opinions? If the LORD is God, follow Him; but if Baal, follow him" (1 Kings 18:21). God would give convincing proof that day that He was Israel's only true God.

So the contest commenced. Throughout the day, the false prophets called on their god to send down fire and consume an animal sacrifice—but to no avail. At the end of the day, Elijah called on Israel's God to send fire to swallow up the sacrifice prepared for Him. God responded to Elijah's prayer. In a moment thousands witnessed the fire from heaven consume the carcass, all the water in the trench and all the wet wood, burning up even the stones!

Elijah exposed the deception of the false prophets of Baal and at last the hearts of the Israelites were convinced that only Israel's God could do this miracle. Elijah then ordered that the false prophets be executed (1 Kings 18:36-40). When the false prophets of Baal were dead, Elijah came under a death threat by Jezebel, the wicked wife of King Ahab. As Israel's queen, she brought the worship of her god Baal into the nation, influencing King Ahab to worship Baal and set up idols in Israel (1 Kings 16:31; 1 Kings 21:25-26). God's prophets who bring messages of warning are often hated and accused of actually being the cause of such suffering. Jezebel and the false prophets of Baal hated Elijah, and they spared no effort to catch him.

In a moment of human weakness Elijah was deeply discouraged, but it wasn't long before God reassured Elijah and sent him back again to face

King Ahab. Elijah was to deliver the message that Ahab and Jezebel would both die a humiliating death because of all the wicked deeds they refused to repent of (1 Kings 21:20-24).

NOTE
The burden...
Our world still has its Ahabs and Jezebels today. The present age also has its idolatry -kind-of-idol-worship, though it is more subtle than that of Elijah's day. The shrines of pagan worship may not be as visible in a basically Christian-professing society, and there may be very few carved images that people actually worship, yet millions are following after the gods of this world. Today's idols can be riches, fame, pleasure and the pleasant-sounding fables that occupy the hearts and minds of many who are unwilling and disinterested in learning about God.

There is need for Elijah-likes to arise in this age, men like John the Baptist who was also a prophet in his time in the spirit and power of Elijah (Luke 1:17) before the coming time of God's great wrath upon the earth. The prophet Malachi declared, "Behold, I will send you Elijah the prophet before the coming of the great and dreadful day of the LORD" (Malachi 4:5-6).

Elijah is considered one of the most important prophets of the Old Testament. He faithfully carried out God's mission in the face of danger and hardship. His was a singular voice of "one crying in the wilderness" to rebuke sin in the land and to expose the false prophets and false religions of his day. In Elijah's day a revival of true worship was begun. Elijah's whole life was devoted to the work of restoring true worship in Israel. His admonition that God's people faithfully serve Him with their whole hearts remains important for us today.

Elijah was a dedicated servant of the Lord in a time when it was very dangerous to even believe in or worship the true God. The whole land in his time was apostate. Of all the thousands of Israel, only seven thousand remained who had not bowed the knee or kissed the hand to Baal. But God is never at a loss. The land may be overrun with sin, the lamps of witness may seem all extinguished, the whole force of the popular current may run counter to His truth, and the plot may threaten to be within a hair's breadth of entire success, but all the time He will be preparing a weak man in some obscure highland village, and in the moment of greatest need will send him forth, as His all-sufficient answer to the worst scheming of His foes. "When the enemy shall come in like a flood, the Spirit of the Lord shall lift up a standard against him" (Isaiah 59:19b). So it has been, and so it shall be again.

Elijah grew up like the other lads of his age. In his early years he probably did the work of a shepherd on those wild hills. As he grew to manhood, his erect figure, his shaggy locks, his cloak of camel's hair, his muscular, sinewy strength-which could out strip the fiery coursers of the royal chariot and endure excessive physical fatigue-distinguished him from the dwellers in lowland valleys. But in none of these would he be particularly different from the men who grew up with him in the obscure mountain hamlet of Tishbe.

As he grew in years, he became characterized by an intense religious earnestness. He was "very jealous for the Lord God of hosts." Deeply taught in Scripture, especially in those passages which told how much Jehovah had done for His people, Elijah yearned, with passionate desire, that they should give Him His honour. And he learned that this was lacking by the dread tidings that came in broken snatches. Messengers after messenger told how Jezebel had thrown down God's altars and slain His prophets and replaced them by the impious rites of her Tyrian deities-his blood ran liquid fire, his indignation burst all bounds, he was "very jealous for the Lord God of hosts." O noble heart! I wish that we could be as righteously indignant amid the evils of our time!

If it can be shown that it was due to something inherent in Elijah and peculiar to himself; some force of nature, some special quality of soul to which ordinary men can lay no claim; then we may as well close our inquiries and turn away from the inaccessible heights that mock us. But if it can be shown, as I think it can, that this splendid life was lived not by its inherent qualities, but by sources of strength which are within the reach of the humblest child of God who reads these lines, then every line of it is an inspiration, beckoning us to its own glorious level. There is nothing in this man's life which may not have its counterpart in ours, if only it can be established that his strength was obtained from sources which are accessible to us.

Elijah's strength did not lie in himself or his surroundings. He was of humble extraction. He had no special training. He is expressly said to have been "a man of like passions" with ourselves. Went through failure of faith, he was cut off from the source of his strength; he showed more craven-hearted cowardice than most men would have done. He lay down upon the desert sands, asking to die. When the natural soil of his nature shows itself, it is not richer than that of the majority of men. If anything it is the reverse.

Elijah prayed, fire fell; people fell and rain fell. How desperate we need heavenly rain because our land is so dry and parched that seed cannot germinate. We need more Elijahs ''who can pray down holy fire in this days. The problem in our time is not lack abilities, talents and gifts. We have too many talents and abilities on display today yet bypassed by God.

In the days of Elijah, Jezebel replaced the priest of God with false deities. She made the people drink iniquity like water. In their days, the salt lost its savour, the gold was dim. Out of this darkness God raise a man-not a committee, not the best of their time, not angel, not a set but a man. The Elijah of this generation could be you!

THE MAN CHARLES G. FINNEY
A GREAT EVANGELIST AND THEOLOGIAN

Charles G. Finney is regarded as the greatest evangelist and theologian since the days of the apostles. It is estimated that during the year 1857-1858 over a hundred thousand persons were led to Christ as the direct or indirect result of Finney's labours, while five hundred thousand persons professed conversion to Christ in the great revival which began in his meetings.

Finney seems to have had the power of impressing the consciences of men with the necessity of holy living in such a manner as to procure the most lasting results. The name of Charles Finney is well-known among students of Revival. After experiencing a thorough Christian conversion he received a powerful infilling of the Holy Spirit and subsequently became an unusually gifted travelling evangelist.

His ministry was largely conducted in local revival campaigns in New York State in the years of 1824-1832. They were in small towns by today's standards, most being less than a thousand in population. The Revival in Rochester in 1842 was the exception. In a population of 10,000 people, around 1,200 were converted, mostly from the educated classes. Charles G. Finney" is perhaps the most remarkable account of the manifestations of the Holy Spirit's power since apostolic days. It is crowded with accounts of spiritual outpourings which tell again one of the days of Pentecost.

Finney's "Systematic Theology" is probably the greatest work on theology outside the Scriptures. The wonderful anointing of God's Spirit, combined with Finney's remarkable reasoning powers and his legal training, enabled him to present clearer views of Christian doctrine than has any other theologian since the days of early Christianity. His views with regard to the difference between physical and moral law and physical and moral depravity, on the reasonableness of the moral law and the atonement, and on the nature of regeneration and sanctification are the clearest of any the writer has had the privilege of reading or hearing.

Charles G. Finney was a descendant of the New England Puritans, and was born in Connecticut in 1792. He moved with his parents to Western New York when two years of age. This part of New York was then a frontier wilderness, with few educational or religious privileges. Finney had a good common school education, however, and at twenty years of age he went to New England to attend high school, but soon afterward went to New Jersey to teach school and to continue his studies. He became quite proficient in Latin, Greek, and Hebrew, and in other college studies. In 1818 he commenced the study of law in the office of Squire Wright, of Adams, near his old home in Western New York.

At Adams, Finney had the first religious privileges worthy of the name. During the three years he taught school in New Jersey, about the only preaching in his neighbourhood was in German, and the preaching he heard while at high school in New England was not of a kind calculated to arrest his attention. The aged preacher he heard there read old manuscript sermons in a monotonous, humdrum way that made no serious impression on the mind of Finney. Finney's parents were not professing Christians, and in his childhood days in Western New York the only preaching he heard was during an occasional visit from some itinerant preacher. At Adams, while studying law, he attended the Presbyterian Church. The pastor, George W. Gale, was an able and highly educated man. His preaching, though of the Old School Calvinistic type, arrested the attention of Finney, although to his keen and logical mind it seemed like a mass of absurdities and contradictions.

It was while studying law and attending church at Adams that Finney became interested in Bible study. He found so many references to the Scriptures in his law books, he decided to buy himself a Bible, and he soon became deeply absorbed in studying it. He had many conversations with Mr Gale, who frequently dropped into the office to talk with him, but they could scarcely agree on any point of doctrine. This fact probably led Finney to study the Scriptures much more diligently than though he had agreed with Mr Gale in everything. The fact that the church members were constantly praying prayers which did not seem to be answered, and to which they hardly seemed to expect an answer, was a great drawback to Finney. But he became more and more concerned about his own soul. He felt that if there was a life beyond he was not prepared for it. Some of the church members wanted to pray for him, but he told them that he did not see that it would do any good because they were continually asking without receiving.

Finney remained in a sceptical yet troubled frame of mind for two or three years. At last he came to a decision that the Bible was the true Word of God, and that it was the fault of the people if their prayers were not answered. He was then brought face to face with the question as to whether or not he would accept Christ. "On a Sabbath evening, in the autumn of 1821," says he, "I made up my mind that I would settle the question of my soul's salvation at once, that if it were possible I would make my peace with God." He was obliged to be in the office, however, and could not devote the entire time to seeking his soul's salvation, although on the following Monday and Tuesday he spent most of his time in prayer and reading the Scriptures. Pride was the great obstacle which hindered him from accepting Christ as his Saviour. He found that he was unwilling that anyone should know that he was seeking salvation. Before praying he stopped the keyhole of the door, and then only prayed in a whisper for fear that someone should hear him. If he was reading the Bible when anyone came in, he would throw his law books on top of it to create the impression that he had been reading them instead of the Bible.

During Monday and Tuesday his conviction of sin increased, but his heart seemed to grow harder. Tuesday night he had become very nervous, and imagined that he was about to die, and sink into hell, but he quieted himself as best he could until morning. Next morning, on the way to the office, he had as clear a view of the atonement of Christ as he ever had afterwards. The Holy Spirit seemed to present Christ: hanging on the cross for him. The vision was so clear that almost unconsciously he stopped in the middle of the street for several minutes when it came to him. North of the village and over a hill laid a piece of woods, or forest, and he decided to go there and pour out his heart in prayer. So great was his pride, he kept out of sight so far as possible for fear that someone should see him on the way to the woods and should think that he was going there to pray.

He penetrated far into the woods where some large trees had fallen across each other leaving an open space between. Into this space he crept to pray. "But when I attempted to pray," says he, "I found that my heart would not pray." He was in great fear lest someone should come and find him praying. He was on the verge of despair, having promised God not to leave the spot until he settled the question of his soul's salvation, and yet it seemed impossible to him to settle the question. "Just at this moment," says he, "I again thought I heard someone approach me, and I opened my eyes to see whether it were so. But right there the revelation of my pride of heart, as the great difficulty that stood in the way, was distinctly shown me.

An overwhelming sense of my wickedness in being ashamed to have a human being see me on my knees before God, took such powerful possession of me, that I cried at the top of my voice, and exclaimed that I would not leave that place if all the men on earth and all the devils in hell surrounded me." He was completely humbled in soul by the thought of his pride. Then the most comforting verses of Scripture seemed to pour into his soul. He saw clearly that faith was not an intellectual state but a voluntary act, and he accepted the promise of God.

Promises of salvation, from both Old and New Testaments, continued to pour into his soul, and he continued to pray. "I prayed," says he, "until my mind became so full that, before I was aware of it, I was on my feet and tripping up the ascent toward the road." On reaching the village he found that it was noon, although he had gone into the woods immediately after an early breakfast. He had been so absorbed in prayer that he had no idea of the time. There was now a great calm in his soul, and the burden of sin had completely rolled away, yet he was tempted to believe that he was not yet born of God. He went to his dinner, but found that he had no appetite. He then went to the office and took down his bass viol, and began to play some hymns, but his soul was so overflowing that he could not sing without weeping.

On the evening of the same day in which Finney received the pardon of his sins, in the manner already described, he received a mighty overwhelming baptism of the Holy Spirit which started him immediately to preaching the gospel. We will allow him to describe this filling of the Spirit in his own words. Continuing the narrative of his conversion, he says:

"After dinner we (Squire Wright and himself) were engaged in removing the books and furniture to another office. We were very busy in this, and had but little conversation all the afternoon. My mind, however, remained in that profoundly tranquil state. There was a great sweetness and tenderness in my thoughts and feelings. Everything appeared to be going right, and nothing seemed to disturb me or ruffle me in the least.

"Just before evening the thought took possession of my mind, that as soon as I was left alone in the new office, I would try to pray again--that I was not going to abandon the subject of religion and give it up, at any rate; and therefore, although I no longer had any concern about my soul, still, I would continue to pray.

"By evening, we got the books and furniture adjusted; and I made up, in an open fire-place, a good fire, hoping to spend the evening alone. Just at dark Squire, seeing that everything was adjusted, bade me good-night and went to his home. I had accompanied him to the door; and as I closed the door and turned around, my heart seemed to be liquid within me. All my feelings seemed to rise and flow out; and the utterance of my heart was, 'I want to pour my whole soul out to God.' The rising of my soul was so great that I rushed into the room back of the front office, to pray.

"There was no fire, and no light, in the room; nevertheless it appeared to me as if it were perfectly light. As I went in and shut the door after me, it seemed as if I met the Lord Jesus Christ face to face. It did not occur to me then, nor did it for some time afterward, that it was wholly a mental state. On the contrary it seemed to me that I saw Him as I would see any other man. He said nothing, but looked at me in such a manner as to break me right down at His feet. I have always since regarded this as a most remarkable state of mind; for it seemed to me a reality, that He stood before me, and I fell down at His feet and poured out my soul to Him. I wept aloud like a child, and made such confession as I could with my choked utterance. It seemed to me that I bathed His feet with my tears; and yet I had no distinct impression that I touched Him, that I recollect.

I must have continued in this state for a good while; but my mind was too much absorbed with the interview to recollect anything that I said. But I know, as soon as my mind became calm enough to break off from the interview, I returned to the front office, and found that the fire that I had made of large wood was nearly burned out. But as I turned and was about to take a seat by the fire, I received a mighty baptism of the Holy Ghost. Without any expectation of it, without ever having the thought in my mind that there was any such thing for me, without any recollection that I had ever heard the thing mentioned by any person in the world, the Holy Ghost descended on me in a manner that seemed to go through me, body and soul. I could feel the impression, like a wave of electricity, going through and through me. Indeed it seemed to come in waves and waves of liquid love; for I could not express it in any other way. It seemed like the very breath of God. I can recollect distinctly that it seemed to fan me, like immense wings.

"No words can express the wonderful love that was shed abroad in my heart. I wept aloud with joy and love; and I do not know but I should say, I literally bellowed out the unutterable gushing of my heart. The waves came over me, and over me, one after the other, until I recollect I cried out, 'I shall die if these waves continue to pass over me.' I said, 'Lord, I cannot bear any more;' yet I had no fear of death."

Finney continued for some time under this remarkable manifestation of the Holy Spirit's power. Wave after wave of spiritual power rolled over him, and through him, thrilling every fibre of his being. Late in the evening a member of his choir--for he was the leader of the choir--came into the office. He was a member of the church, but was astonished to see Finney weeping under the power of the Spirit. After asking a few questions, he went after an elder of the church who was a very serious man, but who laughed with joy when he saw Finney weeping under the Spirit's power. A young man who had associated much with Finney came into the office while Finney was trying to relate his experience to the elder and the member of the choir. He listened with astonishment to what Finney was saying, and suddenly fell upon the floor, crying out in the greatest agony of mind and saying, "Do pray for me!"

Although he had experienced so remarkable a baptism of the Holy Spirit, Finney was tempted the same night, when retiring to bed, to believe that he had been deluded in some way or other, and that he had not received the real baptism of the Spirit. "I soon fell asleep," says he, "but almost as soon woke again on account of the great flow of the love of God that was in my heart. I was so filled with love that I could not sleep. Soon I fell asleep again and awoke in the same manner. When I awoke, this temptation would return upon me and the love that seemed to be in my heart would abate; but as soon as I was asleep it was so warm within me that I would immediately awake. Thus I continued till, late at night, I obtained some sound repose.

"When I awoke in the morning the sun had risen, and was pouring a clear light into my room. Words cannot express the impression that the sunlight made upon me. Instantly the baptism that I had received the night before returned upon me in the same manner. I arose upon my knees in the bed and wept aloud with joy, and remained for some time too much overwhelmed with the baptism of the Spirit to do anything but pour out my soul to God. It seemed as if this morning's baptism was accompanied with a gentle reproof, and the Spirit seemed to say to me, 'Will you doubt?" Will you doubt?' I cried, 'No! I will not doubt; I cannot doubt.' He then cleared the subject up so much to my mind that it was in fact impossible for me to doubt that the Spirit of God had taken possession of my soul."

On the morning just described Finney went to his office, and the waves of power continued to flood his soul. When Squire Wright came into the office, Finney said a few words to him about the salvation of his soul. He made no reply, but dropped his head and went away. Finney says, "I thought no more of it then, but afterward found that the remark I made pierced him like a sword; and he did not recover from it till he was converted."

Almost every person Finney spoke to during the day was stricken with conviction of sin and afterwards found peace with God. His words seemed to pierce their hearts like arrows. Although he had been fond of law, Finney now lost all taste for it and for every other secular business. His whole desire now was to preach the gospel and to win men to Christ. Nothing else seemed of any consequence. He left the office and went out to talk to individuals concerning the salvation of their souls. Among those brought to Christ through his efforts that day were a Universalist and a distiller. During the day there had been much conversation and excitement concerning Finney's conversion, and in the evening most of the people in the village gathered at the church, although no meeting had been appointed so far as Finney could learn. All the people seemed to be waiting for him to speak, and he arose and related what the Lord had done for his soul. A certain Mr C, who was present, was so convicted of sin that he arose and rushed out and went home without his hat. Many others were also deeply-convicted of sin. Finney spoke and prayed with liberty, although he had never prayed in public before. The meeting was a wonderful one, and from that day meetings were held every night for some time. The revival spread among all classes in the village and too many surrounding places. All of Finney's former companions, with one exception, were brought to Christ.

Finney soon visited his home at Henderson, New York, and his parents were brought to Christ. On his return to Adams, he continued his meetings, and spent much time in fasting and prayer. One time as he approached the meeting-house "a light perfectly ineffable" shone in his soul, and almost prostrated him to the ground. It seemed greater than the light of the noon-day sun, as did the light which prostrated Saul on the way to Damascus. He now learned what it was to have real travail of soul for the unsaved. "When Zion travails she shall bring forth" became a precious promise to him.

Finney's first regular meetings were held at Evans Mills, Oneida County, New York. The people praised his sermons, but for two or three weeks no one decided for Christ. Then Finney urged all who were willing to accept Christ to rise to their feet and all who were willing to reject him to remain on their seats. This was very unusual in those days, and made the people so angry that they were almost ready to mob Finney. Next day he spent the day in fasting and prayer, and in the evening preached with such unction and power that a great conviction of sin swept over the people. All night long they were sending for him to come and pray with them. Even hardened atheists were brought to Christ.

He continued to preach the gospel, with increasing power and results, visiting many of the leading cities of America and Great Britain. **Sometimes the power of God was so manifest in his meetings that almost the entire audiences fell on their knees in prayer or were prostrated on the floor. When in the pulpit he sometimes felt almost lifted off his feet by the power of the Spirit of God. Some persons believe that the moral work of the Holy Spirit is not accompanied by any physical manifestations; but both in Bible times and in Finney's meetings remarkable physical manifestations seemed to accompany the moral work of the Holy Spirit when the moral work was deep and powerful. At times, when Finney was speaking, the power of the Spirit seemed to descend like a cloud of glory upon him. Often a hallowed calm, noticeable even to the unsaved, seemed to settle down upon cities where he was holding meetings. Sinners were often brought under conviction of sin almost as soon as they entered these cities.**

Finney seemed so anointed with the Holy Spirit that people were often brought under conviction of sin just by looking at him. When holding meetings at Utica, New York, he visited a large factory there and was looking at the machinery. At the sight of him one of the operatives, and then another, and then another broke down and wept under a sense of their sins, and finally so many were sobbing and weeping that the machinery had to be stopped while Finney pointed them to Christ.

At a country place named Sodom, in the state of New York, Finney gave one address in which he described the condition of Sodom before God destroyed it. "I had not spoken in this strain more than a quarter of an hour," says he, "when an awful solemnity seemed to settle upon them; the congregation began to fall from their seats in every direction, and cried for mercy. If I had had a sword in each hand, I could not have cut them down as fast as they fell. Nearly the whole congregation were either on their knees or prostrate, I should think, in less than two minutes from the first shock that fell upon them. Every one prayed who was able to speak at all." Similar scenes were witnessed in many other places.

In London, England, between 1,500 and 2,000 persons were seeking salvations in one day in Finney's meetings. Enormous numbers inquired the way of salvation in his meetings in New York, Boston, Rochester, and many other important cities of America. The great revival of 1858-1859, one of the greatest revivals in the world's history, was the direct result of his meetings.

Finney's writings have had an enormous circulation and have greatly influenced the religious life of the world. This is especially true of his "Autobiography," his "Lectures on Revivals," "Lectures to Professing Christians," and his "Systematic Theology." These books have all had a worldwide circulation.

Finney continued to preach and to lecture to the students at Oberlin until two weeks before he was eighty-three years of age, when he was called up higher to enjoy the reward of those who have "turned many to righteousness."

THE MAN ORAL ROBERTS
MIRACLES AND HEALING

Miracles are acts of God that proclaim His sovereign power over creation as well as His commitment to the good of His people. Miracle points to God's kingdom and the restoration of creation. During the days of Jesus, He suggests that His miraculous deeds verify that the kingdom of God had come to earth Luke 11: 14-23. Jesus' miracles reveal His divine identity-an identity that calls for worship. This is the response of Jesus after Jesus walks on water: "Truly you are the Son of God" Matthew 14:33. Miracles that God performs through His servants validate the authenticity of the gospel. Ministry without the backing of the power of God to do miracles and to do unusual exploits is an empty ministry.

Join me as we explore the life of this healing evangelist Rev Oral Roberts. Rev Robert was an early pioneer in televangelism, or using television to preach the gospel. His televised faith-healing ministry attracted millions of followers worldwide and made him one of the most recognized religious leaders of the 20th century. In 1954, he brought television cameras into services, providing what he liked to call a "front-row seat to miracles" to viewers. He later began a television program, initially called "Oral Roberts Presents." The ministry's daily program, now called "The Place for Miracles," can be seen on more than 100 television stations, multiple cable and satellite networks and the Internet. Rev Roberts, a stammerer-turned preacher who survived a spell of deadly tuberculosis as an adolescent was the fifth son of a minister in the Pentecostal Holiness church in Pontotoc County, Oklahoma. His childhood was more balanced than many other healing evangelists although he was reared in abject poverty.

Rev Granville Oral Roberts was born January 24, 1918 in Pontotoc County, near Ada, in Oklahoma. His parents were deeply religious. His father was a farmer who also preached the gospel and established Pentecostal Holiness churches. His mother regularly prayed for the sick and led people to Christ. While she was still pregnant, Robert's mother committed Oral to God's service. Even though Oral had a very strong stutter his mother would tell him that one day God would heal his tongue and he would speak to multitudes.

The Roberts family was desperately poor. When Roberts was 16 he moved away from home, hoping for a better life. He rejected God and his upbringing. He started living a wild life and his health collapsed. Roberts had contracted tuberculosis. He returned home and eventually dropped to 120 pounds. He was a walking skeleton. God spoke to his older sister, Jewel, and told her that He was going to heal Oral. During this same time Oral turned his heart back to God and gave his life to Christ. A travelling healing evangelist named George Moncey came to Ada and held meetings in a tent. Oral's elder brother was touched when he saw friends of his healed in the meeting. He decided that he should get Oral and bring him to be healed. On the way to the meeting God spoke to Oral and said "Son, I'm going to heal you and you are to take my healing power to your generation. You are to build me a University and build it on my authority and the Holy Spirit." Once at the meeting Oral waited until the very end. He was too sick to get up and receive prayer, and so had to wait for Moncey to come to him. At 11:00 at night his parents lifted him so he could stand. When Moncey prayed for him the power of God hit him and he was instantly healed. Not only that but every bit of his stutter was gone!

After Roberts was healed he began to travel the evangelistic circuit. He met and married Evelyn Lutman, a school teacher from the same Holiness Pentecostal background as Roberts. They had their first child Rebecca and then the entire family began travelling as ministers. In 1942 they left the evangelistic field for a while and Roberts became a pastor. He also returned to college to further his education. While a pastor he prayed for a church member whose foot was crushed. The foot was instantly healed. God continued to speak to Roberts about his call to the multitudes. God called him to an unusual fast. Roberts was to read the four gospels and the book of Acts three times consecutively, while on his knees, for thirty days. God began to reveal Jesus as the healer in a new way. God also began to give Roberts dreams where he would see people's needs as God saw them. God called him to hold a healing meeting in his town. A woman was dramatically healed, several people were saved and Roberts' ministry changed overnight.

Roberts resigned his church in 1947 and began an itinerant ministry. Notable healings began to occur. One man tried to shoot Roberts. God used the story to bring him media attention, which expanded his ministry very quickly. Roberts felt called to purchase a tent and take his evangelistic ministry to larger cities. His first tent held 3,000 but he quickly exchanged it for a tent that held 12,000. In July 1948 The Oral Roberts Evangelistic Association was established. Oral began travelling continuously throughout the United States. Like many of his Pentecostal brethren he held inter-racial meetings. This brought him a lot of negative attention from groups who didn't like his stand. He even received death threats for not holding segregated meetings. One of these years he held meetings in Sydney and Melbourne. In Melbourne there were outright physical attacks and destructive gangs. He was literally driven out of the city for praying for the sick.

By the end of 1948, Roberts calculated that in ten revivals he "prayed for 50,000 sick" and had 7,000 "saved." In one 1950 campaign in Columbia, South Carolina, there were 13,500 "altar calls." In eleven tent campaigns in 1952, reportedly attended by 1,500,000 people, the organization recorded 66, 000 people prayed for in the healing lines and 38,457 conversions. (Harrell, All Things Are Possible, p44-45)

He rapidly became the exemplary leader of a generation of dynamic revivalists who took the message of divine healing around the world in the 50's. P. G Chappell sums it up so well: 'His ecumenical crusades were instrumental in the revitalization of Pentecostalism in the post-World War II era. He was also influential in the formation of the Full Gospel Business Men's Fellowship International in 1951 as well as a leading figure in laying the foundation for the modern charismatic movement. Roberts' most significant impact upon American Christianity came in 1955 when he initiated a national weekly television program that took his healing crusades inside the homes of millions who had never been exposed to the healing message. Through this program the healing message was literally lifted from the Pentecostal subculture of American Christianity to its widest audience in history. By 1980 a Gallup Poll revealed that Roberts' name was recognized by a phenomenal 84 percent of the American public, and historian Vinson Synan observed that Roberts was considered the most prominent Pentecostal in the world. Oral Roberts (became) the best-known salvation-healing evangelist during the 1950s and 1960s.

In 1965 Roberts opened a coeducational liberal arts college in Tulsa. Oral Roberts University became a major institution when seven graduate colleges were added between 1975 and 1978: Medicine, Nursing, Dentistry, Law,

Business, Education, and Theology. Dedicated in 1967 by Billy Graham, it is considered the premier charismatic university in America. Adjacent to the university Roberts established a 450-resident retirement centre in 1966.

Rev Roberts was a man who understood and used the media for his benefit. He began publishing a magazine almost immediately upon starting his ministry. He grasped the power of radio and television. In 1954 Rev Roberts began filming his crusades. He began playing his sermons on radio and then airing the crusade tapes during evening television prime time. People began writing to the Ministry headquarters by the thousands. They were accepting Christ as their saviour after seeing a person healed on TV. By 1957 the ministry was receiving 1,000 letters a day and he was getting thousands of phone calls. He established a round the clock prayer team to answer calls and pray for people who contacted the ministry. In 1957 Rev Roberts recorded about 1,000,000 salvations. Between 1947 and 1968 Roberts conducted over 300 major Crusades. Money was flowing into the organization at an unprecedented rate.

In 1977 Roberts had a vision to build a hospital where people not only received care but received healing prayer. It was to be called City of Faith. Roberts put his heart and soul into the project, believing that God would build it as He had the University. The hospital was built.

Rev Roberts retired in 1993, at the age of 75. He with his wife Evelyn moved to California to live near the coast. Evelyn died in May 2005. He often appeared on religious broadcasting networks as a recognized leader in the healing movement of the last half century. He died December 15, 2009 at the age of 91.

Rev Roberts' legacy is a mixed one. Roberts brought the truth of God's healing to the public in a way that few others accomplished in his lifetime. "Oral Roberts was a man of God, and a great friend in ministry," the Rev. Billy Graham said. "I loved him as a brother."If God had not in his sovereign raised up the ministry of Oral Roberts, the entire charismatic movement might not have occurred," said Jack Hayford, president of the California-based International Church of the Foursquare Gospel said. "Oral shook the landscape with the inescapable reality and practicality of Jesus' whole ministry. His teaching and concepts were foundational to the renewal that swept through the whole church."

Rev Roberts' monthly magazine, renamed Abundant Life in 1956, reached a circulation of over a million, while his devotional magazine, Daily Blessing, exceeded a quarter million subscribers and a monthly column was written for 674 newspapers. By the 1980s there were more than 15 million copies of his eighty-eight books in circulation, and his yearly mail from supporters exceeded five million letters.

He was the patriarch of the "prosperity gospel," a theology that promotes the idea that Christians who pray and donate with sufficient fervency will be rewarded with health, wealth and happiness. Rev Roberts trained and mentored several generations of younger prosperity gospel preachers who now have television and multimedia empires of their own. By 1985, the Oral Roberts Evangelistic Association and Oral Roberts University employed more than 2,300 people.

Theologically Roberts is basically a classical Pentecostal, who maintains that speaking in tongues is normative for every believer. His trademark, however, has been essentially an upbeat message of hope. The whole thesis of his ministry has been that God is a good God and that He wills to heal and prosper His people (3 John 2).

The anointing and authority God gave to these early fathers and mothers did not leave when they departed. God's commission remained when Elijah left, falling on Elisha. The mandate was transferable. What made Elijah a great prophet, and what made Elisha a great prophet, was what made John the Baptist a great prophet too. But that was not the last of the matter. What made the Early Men: John Knox, Apostle Joseph Ayo Babalola, John G. Lake, Kathryn Kuhlman, Benson Idahosa, Smith Wigglesworth, Stephen, Moody D. L., William Seymour, Elijah, Charles G. Finney, Rev Oral Roberts, Noah, Aimee SempleMcpherson, John Wesley, Martin Luther, John Wycliffe, T. L. Osborn, Charles Spurgeon, Pa Josiah Akindayomi, Maria Woodworth-Etter, Parham, Charles Fox and Evan Roberts great men and women of God, the Apostles great; the same Spirit is here.

The same Spirit who was upon these great servants is still here and we are included in His Company. The Spirit that rested on the early men and women has never left. He is here and will still remain generations yet to come if Jesus tarries His coming. We are in God's revival team, right alongside all these early men and women, the martyrs and the Apostles. We share the platform with them all. What belonged to the great men and women of God in the past is ours and what is ours today was once theirs.

These men who shook the world with the power of God had gone. Men and women of the historic revival had all gone except the Chief Corner Stone, Jesus Christ. He is here! He is with us! He is still baptizing into the Holy Spirit.

THE WOMAN MARIA WOODWORTH-ETTER
"GRANDMOTHER OF THE PENTECOSTAL MOVEMENT"

Our generation appears sleeping. In some quarters, it has been a slumber of many. In one sense my generation's slumber is not universally. Never in God's agenda has He not one awake for Him! Multitude may be sleeping but there is always little flock or a man awake. Even in the world's deepest midnight there have been always children of the light and of the day. In the midst of a slumbering world some have been in every age awake.

The page before us contains the story a woman God found useable in the midst of almost lost age. Maria was born in New Lisbon, Ohio, on July 22, 1844 to Samuel Lewis and Matilda Britain Underwood. She was the fourth daughter of Samuel and Matilda Underwood, one of eight children. Opportunity for Maria to attend church was rare. Maria's parents weren't believers and education was limited to memorizing an occasional verse. Being raised with seven siblings, an alcoholic father and a sickly broken hearted mother, her youth was very hard. When she was only eight years old she felt a strong desire to know God, and when Maria's older sisters were converted in a Methodist meeting, her heart "was melted in the Saviour's love." However Maria was denied because children at her age were considered too young to profess salvation.

Her first loss occurred in 1857 when her father went out to the field to work but was carried back to the house with a severe case of sunstroke. Her mother was left with eight children and no support. Her mother and all the children old enough had to work to support the family. Her father finally died and the family experienced deep sorrow and deeper poverty. Maria and her sisters worked during the week to provide for the large impoverished family. Maria couldn't attend school since her mother needed her to work. She cried herself to sleep at night while living and working away from home.

Maria Woodworth–Etter was a painfully timid woman, uneducated, isolated much of the time, sickly and poor. In human wildest imaginations she couldn't be considered as an instrument in the Hand of God. When she heard the gospel preached at church, she was very moved by it and decided that she wanted to be a Christian. At age thirteen Maria was converted. This happened not at going forward at a meeting, but the next day at her water baptism where she asked the Lord to save her fully.

At that point she experienced a light that came over her, and some folks said she fainted. Soon after conversion Maria's new joy in salvation consumed her. She went to as many as seven or eight church meetings a week but had no interest in amusement. At this time her longstanding desire for an education was intensified especially since she'd heard the voice of Jesus calling her to go out in the highways and hedges and gather in the lost sheep. Maria never heard of any woman preaching. She rationalized that with an education and a husband they might be accepted for missions work. A few years later she married her Philo Harris Woodworth. They attempted to farm but it was a failure. They settled out in a country place where opportunity for church attendance was nonexistent. Maria's hopes died.

The future, however, had some unexpected turns. Maria's (now Mrs. Woodworth) health had failed and although she longed to attend church, she was not able. From her bed she would hear the church bells ringing and would cry herself to sleep. Not only did her health fail, but the health of her son did also. As he lay dying, he said to Woodworth, "Mamma, do not weep for me; I am going to a better world." Woodworth said these words, "It almost broke my heart to lay him away in the cold grave; but I could see the loving hands of God and hear Him calling me to build up higher, to set my affections on heavenly things and not on things of the earth."

The tragedy was repeated a year later as Woodworth's baby, Freddy, was taken by death as well. Around this time, Woodworth's seven-year old daughter, Georgie, was converted. Sadly, she developed the disease, scrofula, and suffered painfully from its effects. She sent messages to her Sunday school teacher, fellow students and friends telling them to meet her in heaven. One day, after eight months of struggling with the disease, she said to Woodworth, "Mamma, I'm going to leave you this week." On the last day of that week, Georgie died. As she was passing, she said to Woodworth, "O Mamma, I see Jesus and the angels; I see my little brothers; they have come for me." Woodworth said, "It was like death to part with my darling. But Jesus was very precious to my soul. Heaven was nearer; Christ was dearer than ever before. I had one more treasure in glory." Three weeks before Georgie died, Woodworth had given birth to a girl, Gertie. Gertie lived for only four months and died also.

Heaven and Christ were nearer than ever to Woodworth as she herself hung between life and death. During this time, she had a number of visions. She would see heaven. She would also see herself pleading with sinners to come to Jesus. God was again calling her to the work of the ministry. Woodworth wrestled with not wanting to fulfil her calling. Part of her wanted to die and go to be with the Lord and with her children who had passed on. However, she promised the Lord that if He would restore her health and prepare her for the work that she must do, she would endeavour to accomplish it. Immediately, her health began to recover.

Even after making this commitment to the Lord, she feared stepping out into the work. The Lord gave her a very sobering vision. She says: "Then the Lord, in a vision, caused me to see the bottomless pit, open in all its horror and woe. There was weeping and wailing and gnashing of teeth. It was surrounded by a great multitude of people who seemed unconscious of their danger; and without a moments warning, they would tumble into this awful place. I was above the people on a narrow plank-walk, which wound up toward heaven; and I was exhorting and pleading with the people to come up onto the plank and escape that awful place. Several started. There was a beautiful bright light above me, and I was encouraging them to follow that light and they would go straight to heaven."

This vision deeply impressed upon her the responsibility of her calling. More sorrows were ahead for Woodworth. This time her six-year old son, Willie, became ill. He knew that he was not going to recover and told Woodworth and the others that he was going to be with Jesus. He soon died. Woodworth said. He was the joy of my life, nearly seven years old. He was very bright for one of his age—in fact, far beyond his years. He was the pet of the whole neighbourhood … This sad bereavement nearly took my life. The dear Saviour was never so near and real to me before. He was by my side and seemed to bear me up in His loving arms. I could say, "the LORD gave and the [LORD hath] taken away; blessed be the name of the [LORD]."

By His grace, the Lord carried Woodworth through experiences such as this. Woodworth now had one remaining daughter, sixteen year old Lizzie. The Lord's grace was about to show itself in another way. Woodworth says that she felt unqualified for the work that she was called to do. In simple faith, she asked the Lord to anoint her for service. In answer to this prayer, she had a wonderful experience. She says: The power of The Holy Ghost came down as a cloud. It was brighter than the sun. I was covered and wrapped up in it. My body was as light as the air. It seemed that heaven came down. I was baptized with the Holy Ghost and fire and power, which have never left me. Oh praise The Lord! There was liquid fire, and the angels were all around and the fire and the glory. It is through the Lord Jesus Christ and by this power that I have stood before hundreds of thousands of men and women, proclaiming the unsearchable riches of Christ.

The time had come; Woodworth stepped out in faith. She held a small meeting in her home town and began preaching on the text "… Set thine house in order; for thou shalt die, and not live." (2 Kings 20.1; and see Isaiah 38.1). As she was preaching, all fear of man left her and her words rang with greater and greater conviction. She continued holding meetings for a few days and twenty souls were converted. Encouraged by this, she held more meetings and, when preaching, she experienced the same power that she had received when she was baptized in the Holy Ghost. The glory of God seemed to descend and fill the meeting houses.

Maria Woodworth-Etter was undoubtedly the most successful female evangelist of the early 20th Century. She attracted as many as 25,000 to a single service, and she crossed the country filling churches, halls, and tents with seeking souls. Her meetings were marked by the manifestations that many associated with frontier revivals of the early 19th Century, and her pulpit persona was commanding. A front-page New York Times article from January 1885, detailed some of the "strange scenes" at meetings held in Hartford City, Indiana: "Scores have been stricken down at these meetings, and whatever forms the limbs or body chance to assume in that position, immovable as a statue, they remained " Further, the newspaper described the revival's charismatic leader: "The lady evangelist, Mrs. Woodworth, is a lady of fine physique, comely, and of a commanding appearance, and while not highly cultured and refined yet she is an impressive speaker, and when speaking keeps her hands in constant motion." During the meeting, she was also subject to the ecstatic catalepsy and trances, which became a trademark of her campaigns. It is not at all clear when Maria Woodworth-Etter received the baptism of the Holy Ghost, speaking in tongues, but she seems to have accepted the sign of the baptism, though she had no direct association with the Pentecostal Movement before the protracted revival in Dallas in 1912.

After a rather quiet period 1904 to 1912, Maria hit the sawdust trail with the vigour she demonstrated in her 1880s campaigns. The role Maria played between 1912 and her death in 1924 is unique, providing a veteran "name" evangelist for the young Movement. Pentecostals called for her from all over the country. Others around the world read her books that reported high-powered meetings, remarkable conversions, healings, and a great number of church plantings. In addition, Maria used books to publish her sermons.

One of the calls she accepted came from Fred F. Bosworth, a young pastor in Dallas, who later became a well-known evangelist himself. Despite the fact that the 1912 meeting proved to be a key Pentecostal meeting, the Dallas newspapers practically ignored the thousands who were meeting daily and nightly for almost 5 months. Bosworth, however, kept the news flowing into Christian publications around the world.

R.J. Scott, a Christian businessman associated with the Azusa Street Mission, travelled to Dallas to check out Maria's Pentecostal ministry. He liked what he heard and invited her as the main speaker for the Worldwide Camp Meeting he was planning for the spring of 1913 at Arroyo Seco, near Pasadena.

The Woodworth-Etter train rolled into Chicago late in 1913, and several Pentecostal missions cooperated with the Stone Church in a campaign. Anna C. Reiff, editor of the Latter Rain Evangel and former secretary to John Alexander Dowie, described the meetings as Chicago's "mightiest visitation of the supernatural she has ever known." Evangelist A.H. Argue echoed that remark, stating it was the "mightiest visitation from God of these latter days."

In one of Woodworth's meetings in Atlanta a woman who had been born deaf and dumb was healed. Overwhelmed with joy, she began to dance and went over to a piano which was being played. She was hearing music for the first time in her life and was very much affected by the sound of it.

Another one to be deeply affected was an alcoholic man who came to one of Woodworth's tent meetings in Massachusetts. He had an encounter with God, was saved, healed from several chronic ailments and permanently delivered from alcoholism. He returned home to Connecticut a completely changed man. The next morning, he was baptized in the Holy Spirit and was speaking in tongues. In a few months, all the members of his family who were old enough to understand were baptized in the Holy Spirit. Seven of his ten living children attended Bible College, five married ministers and two became missionaries. Six of the grandchildren also went on to full-time ministry.

At age seventy-four, Etter continued to be very active, by this time, she had a permanent tabernacle set up at Indianapolis. She continued to travel as well, drawing crowds of one to two thousand. In 1924, at eighty years of age, after fifty years of ministry, Etter died peacefully in her room. She died without a struggle and with the respect of thousands.

The lives of five of her children were taken. Her own health was brought low on repeated occasions. She was misunderstood by many and misjudged as insane. Newspapers maligned her. Police arrested her. Courts tried her. Yet in these situations, Mrs. Woodworth-Etter was courageous, unshakeable and ultimately victorious in her high calling and mission to walk in revival and to lead multitudes to faith in Christ. The word of the Lord went before her and a stream of healing followed behind her. She lived and walked in the realm of revival faith where heaven is real, deliverance is real, hope is real and Jesus is all in all. With the anointing of the Lord, the simple faith of a child, and with a heart as large as her tent, she carried the good news of salvation and healing to multitudes of needy, searching souls.

"The power which was given to the apostles in their day had never been taken from the church. The trouble was, the churches had sunk to the level of the world and were without the unlimited faith that will heal the sick and make the lame to walk. She prayed for the return of the old days and more faith in Christ among the people." **Woodworth Etter**

What a life! No matter how dark or spiritually dead this generation may appear to be, God is raising some combustible vessels that will carry fire and walk in the fire of His presence. While Jesus ministered on earth, His greatest passion was to release the fire of God's presence. **"I have come to bring fire on the earth, and how I wish it were already kindled" Luke 12:49**.

If my generation must do well, we need this fire that only Jesus brings. We will be talking about this fire later in this book. If we receive this fire Jesus brought, our heart, ministry, family and world will change-transform. Some of us are good a discussing theology, but we often lose our arguments because of fire-less-ness. God did not call you and I to argue but to testify Him to our world in power and vigour-what we have seen, heard and experienced.

How we need this fire in this generation. Fellowship in the fire! God made you and I flame of fire. How we desperately we need fire carriers. Brethren, it is this fire that makes the difference. Help make our Lord's desire in **Luke 12:49** "I have come to bring fire on the earth, **AND HOW I WISH IT WERE ALREADY KINDLED**." We will only be weakening cowards without this fire. If this fire comes, nothing can intimidate us or stop us.

If this fire comes on us, we will be turned into another people. This fire, when it comes on an ordinary animal, that animal will harass and conquer a nation. God through Sampson converted animal into combustible fire carriers.

"So he went out and caught three hundred foxes and tied them tail to tail in pairs. Lit the torches and let the foxes loose in the standing corn of the Philistines. He burned up the shocks and standing corn, together with the vineyards and olive groves." Judges 15:4-5

But we are better, stronger and more capable than these animals. If you and I will avail ourselves to catch this fire, we will do much more for God!

THE MAN PARHAM, CHARLES FOX
FOUNDER OF THE APOSTOLIC FAITH MOVEMENT

Charles Fox Parham, the 'father of the Pentecostal' Movement, is most well known for perceiving, proclaiming and then imparting the 'The Baptism with the Holy Spirit with the initial evidence of speaking in other tongues.' He was born in Muscatine, Iowa on June 4, 1873 to the family of William and Ann Parham. Charles's mother was a devout Christian and she died in 1885, which was a devastating blow to him.

Charles Fox Parham, in 1878, William, a house painter and horse-collar maker, moved the family by prairie schooner south and settled in Kansas. Shrewdly investing his money in agriculture, he won for his family a comfortable living on their 160-acre farm near Anness, Kansas. But young Charles wrestled with poor health, ranging from infant encephalitis to tapeworms. To make matters worse, he contracted rheumatic fever at age 9, which weakened his heart and forced him into long periods of inactivity. Once, he nearly died from a recurrence.

Although the Parham family made no particular confession of faith, his mother taught him the value of godly devotion. Charles was converted in 1886 when he attended evangelistic meetings at a local Congregational church; a "Damascus road" experience that changed the direction of his life. Shortly afterward, Parham began attending a Methodist church where he taught Sunday school.

At age 15, he began conducting revival services on his own. To further prepare himself for ministry, in 1890, he enrolled at Southwest Kansas College in Winfield. While a student, Parham "backslid" and decided to become a medical doctor. But following another stretch with rheumatic fever, he recommitted himself to the ministry. Returning to evangelistic work, he obtained a minister's license from the Southwest Kansas Conference of the Methodist Episcopal Church, North. At age 20, he received a temporary appointment as supply pastor at the Eudora

Methodist Church near Lawrence, Kansas.

Despite his successful ministry among the people, Parham's relationship with his Methodist superiors became tense. His ambiguous attitude toward denominational affiliation did not warm their hearts. More importantly, Parham's adoption of Wesleyan "holiness" theology with its crisis experience of sanctification branded him as a troublemaker. Holiness preachers declared that following conversion, believers should seek for this "second blessing" to purge the Adamic nature from their hearts. To Methodist leaders, this smacked of doctrinal aberration. By 1895, Parham broke with Methodism—in fact, all denominationalism—for good. He started his own independent evangelical ministry in Kansas, where he held revival meetings that emphasized personal salvation. He also advocated a return to the fundamental teachings of the scriptures, or "primitive Christianity."

At the annual Southwest Kansas district conference in 1895, Parham surrendered his license to preach and "left denominationalism forever." Denouncing Methodism as spiritually bankrupt, he had a "world-wide parish," free of the "confines of a pastorate, with a lot of theatre-going, card-playing, wine-drinking, fashionable, unconverted Methodists." Though freedom from denominational restraints offered Parham the liberty he desired, it brought new problems, uncertainties, and hardships. Nevertheless, he found a measure of success.

Before long, he was overcome by an exhaustive preaching schedule and suffered once more from a heart ailment possibly related to his struggle with rheumatic fever. In 1886, he married Sarah Thistlethwaite, the daughter of a devout Quaker family. A son born to them some time later became deathly ill. After pleading with God for their healing, Parham testified to their complete recovery. Praying for the sick then became a featured part of his ministry and like other advocates of the period, he challenged the medical profession: "The [Bible] is significantly silent about any ministry of pills or powders."

As his ministry gained more recognition, Parham moved his family and base of operations to Topeka, Kansas, in 1898. There he founded Bethel Healing Home and enlarged his activities to include rescue missions for prostitutes and the homeless, an employment bureau, an orphanage service, and later a Bible institute. To highlight these enterprises, he began publishing a holiness periodical, the Apostolic Faith.

By this time, Parham's teachings included divine healing, the crisis view of sanctification, and belief in the imminent return of Christ. Something else now drew his attention: the baptism in the Holy Spirit. Mainline holiness believers at the end of the 19th century referred to sanctification as baptism in the Spirit, an ushering in of a higher stage of Christian living providing purification and empowerment. However, on the radical holiness circuit, Benjamin Hardin Irwin taught the "fire-baptized" doctrine of a third experience of grace. Critics called it the "third blessing heresy." To Irwin, as well as Parham who endorsed it, sanctification cleansed believers as vessels for the Master's use (2 Timothy 2:21), and only afterward could the Spirit pour in His power. Naturally, this created a dilemma: How could one distinguish the evidence of Spirit baptism from the fruit of sanctification?

Even with Parham's oratorical skills and the expansion of his ministry in Topeka, his efforts there had largely failed and disillusionment swept over him. His need for a fresh vision led him to the Holy Ghost and Us Bible School at Shiloh, Maine. Radical evangelicals on the fringe of the missions movement uniquely contended that supernatural "signs and wonders" (Acts 5:12) should accompany the preaching of the gospel according to Matthew 10:5—10 and Mark 16:17, 18. With the close of human history fast approaching, only a mighty intervention of the Spirit's power could ensure that every tribe and nation would hear the good news in time (Matthew 24:14).

As Parham's theology of baptism in the Holy Spirit evolved, he concluded that recipients would form an elite band of end-times missionaries with supernatural power to evangelize the world. In fact, "missionary tongues" not only resolved the evidence question of the Pentecostal baptism, but bestowed immediate readiness for missionaries by eliminating their need to spend months or years in language school before they could preach in their countries of service. After all, Jesus had said: "And these signs shall follow them that believe they shall speak with new tongues" (Mark 16:17). Significantly, Parham recalled hearing speaking in tongues for the first time at Shiloh as he listened to students coming down from the prayer tower after hours of intercession. To Sandford, tongues simply represented an occasional revival phenomenon.

There were recent precedents of persons suddenly receiving the capacity to preach in other languages. In 1881, a missionary to India, Miss C.M. Reade, testified of the Spirit's giving her the "gift of speaking Hindustani" to enable her to preach without a translator. Similar reports came from Jonathan Goforth, the famed Canadian Presbyterian missionary to China, as well as W.P. Buncombe, an Anglican serving in Japan. Yet it is doubtful that Parham knew about them.

Others, however, found only disappointment. While it remains uncertain if Parham had heard of these failed attempts, the testimony of a young Missourian, Jennie Glassey, impressed him deeply. He reprinted a brief account in the May 1899 edition of the Apostolic Faith. According to the story, she "received the African dialect in one night while in the Spirit in 1895, but could read and write, translate and sing the language while out of the trance or in a normal condition, and can until now. Hundreds of people can testify to the fact, both saint and sinner, who heard her, use the language. She was also tested in Liverpool and Jerusalem. Her Christian experience is that of a holy, consecrated woman, filled with the Holy Ghost."

Now revitalized, Parham returned to Kansas and started his own Bible school in October 1900. Calling it the Bethel Healing Home, he modelled it in part after Sandford's school, and he taught college-age students the need for a restoration of New Testament Christianity, or a return to "primitive Christianity." Biblical truth, Parham preached, could be gained only by returning to the teachings of the Apostles and following the words found in the Book of Acts. That part of the Bible, Parham believed, was where the true word of God was found. Parham eventually expanded his theology to include the laying of hands on others during prayer, speaking in tongues, and baptism of the Holy Spirit, which led to purification of the soul. Religious historians regard the opening of Parham's Bible school as the birth of modern Pentecostalism.

After this incredible deluge of the Holy Spirit, the students moved their beds from the upper dormitory on the upper floor and waited on God for two nights and three days, as an entire body.

On the night of January 3rd 1901, Parham preached at a Free Methodist Church in Topeka, telling them what had happened and that he expected the entire school to be baptized in the Holy Spirit. On returning to the school with one of the students they heard the most wonderful sounds coming from the prayer room. "The room was filled with shine of white light above the brightness of the lamps." There were twelve denominational ministers who had received the Holy Spirit baptism and were speaking in other tongues. Some were gently trembling under the power of the glory that had filled them. Sister Stanley, an elderly lady, came to Parham, and shared that she saw "tongues of fire" sitting above their heads just moments before his arrival.

"My heart was melted in gratitude to God for my eyes had seen. I fell to my knees behind a table unnoticed by those on whom the power of Pentecost had fallen to pour out my heart to God in thanksgiving" Then he asked God for the same blessing, and when he did, Parham distinctly heard God's calling to declare "this mighty truth to the world. And if I was willing to stand for it, with all the persecutions, hardships, trials, slander, scandal that it would entailed, He would give me the blessing." It was then that Charles Parham himself was filled with the Holy Spirit, and spoke in other tongues. "Right then and there came a slight twist in my throat, a glory fell over me and I began to worship God in a Swedish tongue, which later changed to other languages and continued so until the morning"

Within a few days about half the student body had received the Holy Spirit with the evidence of tongues. Soon the news of what God was doing had Stone's Folly besieged by newspaper reporters, language professors, foreigners and government interpreters and they gave the work the most crucial test. They had to agree that Stone's Folly's students were speaking in the languages of the world, with the proper accent and intonation. The newspapers broadcast the headlines "Pentecost! Pentecost!! Pentecost!!!"

On January 21, 1901, Parham preached the first sermon dedicated to the sole experience of the baptism of the Holy Spirit with the evidence of speaking in other tongues at the Academy of music in Kansas City. According to accounts, within a few days, Parham and about half the students also underwent the same experience. Parham maintained that this sudden collective ability was directly attributable to God. Parham termed the ability to speak in tongues as "xenoglossae," which means "foreign tongues" in Greek. The reason God provided this gift, he said, was to allow true believers to go out into all parts of the world and save souls without having to learn a foreign language. In the wake of this collective experience, Parham founded a new movement called the "Apostolic Faith."

In the autumn of 1903, the Parham's moved to Galena, Kansas, and began meeting in a supporter's home. Large crowds caused them to erect a large tent which, though it seated two thousand people, was still too small to accommodate the crowds. The blind, lame, deaf and all manner of diseases were marvellously healed and great numbers saved. As winter approached a building was located, but even then, the doors had to be left open during services to include the crowds outside.

The message of Pentecostal baptism with tongues, combined with divine healing, produced a surge of faith and miracles, rapidly drawing massive support for Parham and the Apostolic Faith movement. The St. Louis Globe reported 500 converts, 250 baptized in water and "Blindness and

Cancer Cured". Late that year successful ministry was conducted at Joplin, Missouri, and the same mighty power of God was manifested. Blind eyes were opened, the sick were healed and many testified of conversion and sanctification by the Spirit. Many more received the Spirit according to Acts 2:4. The meetings continued four weeks and then moved to a building for many more weeks with revival scenes continuing. So great was the strain that Parham was taken sick with exhaustion and, though near death at one point, he was miraculously raised up through the prayer of faith.

On March 21st 1905, Parham travelled to Orchard, Texas, in response to popular requests from some who had been blessed at Kansas meetings. When ministering in Orchard, there was such a great outpouring of the Spirit, that the entire community was transformed.

From Orchard Parham left to lay siege to Houston, Texas, with twenty-five dedicated workers. It was July 10th 1905. "Non-denominational" meetings were held at Bryan Hall, anyone who wanted to experience more of the power of God was welcomed. Parham's interest in the Holy land became a feature in his meetings and the press made much of this and generally wrote favourably of all the healings and miracles that occurred.

After the meetings, Parham and his group held large parades, marching down the streets of Houston in their Holy Land garments. These parades attracted many to the evening services. Extraordinary miracles and Holy Ghost scenes were witnessed by thousands in these meetings.

During these months a string of Apostolic Faith churches were planted in the developing suburbs of Houston, despite growing hostility and personal attacks.

Undaunted by the persecution, Parham moved on to Galveston in October 1905, holding another powerful campaign. Soon after the family moved to Houston, believing that the Holy Spirit was leading them to locate their headquarters and a new Bible school in that city. As at Topeka, the school was financed by freewill offerings. No tuition was charged and each student had to exercise faith for his or her own support. The school opened in December 1905 and each course was ten weeks in duration.

"This was not a 'Theological seminary' but a place where the great essential truths of God were taught in the most practical manner to reach the sinner, the careless Christian, the backslider and all in need of the gospel message."

It was here that Parham first met William J. Seymour, a black Holiness evangelist. The 'Jim Crow' laws forbad blacks and whites from mixing, and attending school together was prohibited. But Seymour's humility and deep interest in studying the Word so persuaded Parham that he decided to offer Seymour a place in the school. Seymour subsequently carried the new Pentecostal message back to Los Angeles, where through the Azusa Street revival; he carried on the torch, winning many thousands of Pentecostal converts from the U.S. and various parts of the world.

Parham was at the height of his popularity and enjoyed between 8-10,000 followers at this time. He was in great demand. The work was growing apace everywhere, not least of all in Los Angeles, to which he sent five more workers. Sensing the growing momentum of the work at Azusa Street, Seymour wrote to Parham requesting help. He planned to hire a larger building to give full exposure to Parham's anointed ministry and believed that it would "shake the city once more" with a spiritual "earthquake." Seymour also needed help with handling spurious manifestations that were increasing in the meetings. He wrote "urgent letters appealing for help, as spiritualistic manifestations, hypnotic forces and fleshly contortions had broken loose in the meetings. He wanted Parham to come quickly and help him discern between that which was real and that which was false." Unfortunately, Parham failed to perceive the potential of the Los Angeles outpouring and continued his efforts in the mid-west, which was the main centre of his 'Apostolic Faith' movement. The Azusa Street spiritual earthquake happened without him.

The Apostolic Faith, revived the previous year, became thoroughly Pentecostal in outlook and theology and Parham began an attempt to link the scattered missions and churches. Adopting the name 'Projector' he formulated the assemblies into a loose-knit federation of assemblies – quite a change in style and completely different from his initial abhorrence of organised religion and denominationalism. He also encouraged "Assembly meetings," weekly meetings of twenty or thirty workers for prayer, sharing and discussion, each with its own designated leader or pastor. Soon he announced the ordination of elders in each major town and the appointment of three state directors. Parham was clearly making efforts to ensure the movement's continuance and progress.

Parham arrived Zion but at first, it was impossible to obtain a building for the meetings. He secured a private room at the Elijah Hospice (hotel) for initial meeting and soon the place was overcrowded. Soon Parham began cottage meetings in many of the best homes of the city. One of these homes belonged to the great healing evangelist and author, F. F. Bosworth. Every night five different meetings were held in five different homes, which lasted from 7:00 p.m. till midnight. When his workers arrived, he would preach from meeting to meeting, driving rapidly to each venue. "Hundreds of backsliders were reclaimed, marvellous healings took place and Pentecost fell profusely."

In October of 1906, Parham felt released from Zion and hurried to Los Angeles to answer Seymour's repeated request for help. He was shocked at what he found. "To my utter surprise and astonishment I found conditions even worse that I had anticipated. I saw manifestations of the flesh, spiritualistic controls, and people practicing hypnotism at the altar over people seeking the baptism; though many were receiving the real Baptism of the Holy Spirit."

In analyzing the life and legacy of any Christian, it is important to remember Paul's counsel to the Corinthian believers: "We have this treasure in jars of clay to show that this all-surpassing power is from God and not from us" (2 Corinthians 4:7, NIV). Students of history should neither glorify Parham beyond his actual achievements nor dismiss his memory. In God's mercy, He uses frail human beings.

Parham went to be with the Lord on January 29, 1929 at the age of 56 and he received his "Well done, good and faithful servant" from the Lord he loved. Over twenty-five hundred people attended his funeral at the Baxter Theatre. It took over an hour for the great crowd to pass the open casket for their last view of this gift of God to His church. A choir of fifty occupied the stage, along with a number of ministers from different parts of the nation. Over his casket people who had been healed and blessed under his ministry wept with appreciation. Offerings were sent from all over the United States to help purchase a monument. The family chose a granite pulpit with an open Bible on the top on which was carved "John 15:13," which was his last sermon text, "Greater love hath no man than this, that a man lay down his life for his friends."

It is estimated that Charles Parham's ministry contributed to over two million conversions, directly or indirectly. His congregations often exceeded seven thousand people and he left a string of vibrant churches that embraced Pentecostal doctrines and practices. In addition he fathered three sons, all of whom entered the ministry and were faithful to God, taking up the baton their father had passed to them. But his greatest legacy was as the "father of the Pentecostal movement." No other person did more than him to proclaim the truth of speaking in tongues as the evidence of the baptism of the Holy Spirit.

His passion for souls, zeal for missions, and his eschatological hopes helped frame early Pentecostal beliefs and behavior. He managed to marry a prevailing holiness theology with a fresh, dynamic and accessible ministry of the Holy Spirit, which included divine healing and spiritual gifts. Charles Fox Parham will forever be one of the bright lights in God's hall of fame, characterized by a dogged determination and relentless pursuit of God's best and for God's glory. Despite personal sickness and physical weakness, continual persecution and unjustified accusation this servant of God was faithful to the heavenly vision and did his part in serving the purpose of God in his generation. May we be as faithful, expectant, hard-working and single-minded!

THE MAN EVAN ROBERTS
THE MAJOR FIGURE FOR WALES'S AWAKENING

Evan Roberts is the fundamental figure of the religious awakening in Wales. He is an illustration of spiritual misfits (the unqualified, unprofessional, ill equip and amateur) that God often uses to bring revival or establish His mandate in the affairs of men. Roberts was a 26-year-old who had dropped out of Bible school to go home and pray for revival. "Day and night without ceasing, he prayed, wept and sighed for a great spiritual awakening. Like many of God's instruments of revival, Evan Roberts was not a great orator or brilliant theologian. But he did know how to obey the promptings of the Holy Spirit.

Often when trying to pray or preach, he became so overwhelmed by the Spirit he couldn't speak. He would collapse behind the pulpit and sob like a baby. Then the Holy Spirit would sweep through the congregation and people would begin to spontaneously confess their sins. Others, convicted by those confessions, would then stream down the aisles and come to Christ. He was proof that God is able to do much more through much less, when a heart is fully surrendered to the Holy Spirit!

God does not use people because they are perfect or talented, He uses people because they yield to Him. He is always asking: whom shall I send? Our being used by God is termed a reasonable service. The fact that God uses men at all is a wonderful reality. From one point of view He doesn't need us. As Jesus once said, He could use stones if He wished, but He has chosen to use men. This means, of course, that He has chosen to use imperfect instruments. Yet our imperfection will not block God if our attitudes are such that we are willing to be used by Him.

When God reached Naaman He did it through "a young girl" (2 Kings 5:2). When God wanted to lead Saul of Tarsus into the assurance of salvation He used Ananias. But who was he? He was a disciple (Acts 9:10)- not an apostle, not an outstanding man, and not necessarily a leader. The fact that God delights to use ordinary people should be a great encouragement to many.

Evan Roberts was born of very godly devout and hard working parents in 1878. He was one of 14 children and one of seven sons. Their home, called "Island House" was situated on the banks of the river Llwchwr in Loughor, a small village in Glamorgan in South Wales. Near Loughor was the coal mine where he went to work with his father. He was just 11 years old at the time which of course brought an end to his school education. He was a 'door boy' which entailed opening and closing doors for the drams carrying coal up and down the shafts. The old Welsh preachers would refer to those dark and dangerous mines as a picture of Hell or the darkness of men's depraved hearts, to which those like Evan who worked down underground, could well relate.

From his earliest days Evan was of a most serious and solemn nature. He was a constant student of the Bible and was never found without it, either in his hand or pocket. Once in an explosion in the mine his Bible was scorched but Evan was unharmed. When manning these mine doors he would often give the passing miners a written text of scripture to meditate on and would later ask them what they had learned. This boy intended to be a preacher. His separation from all the boyish fun of others of his age around him was just a mark of how serious he was about this. He had no outstanding gift to speak or expound the scripture that anyone could see, but the blamelessness of his life was apparent to all.

He faithfully attended every weekly meeting at Moriah Chapel, the large Calvinistic Methodist church which his family attended. Moriah was one of several Nonconformist chapels in Loughor. After an Elder challenged young Evan concerning faithfulness in attending God's House he made it his habit to attend without fail. The Elder had queried how Evan would feel if he were absent when the Spirit of God fell, so there was not a night of the week when he was not at some meeting. In 1902 he left work in the mine and began an apprenticeship with his uncle as a Blacksmith going about his business faithfully and almost un-noticed, but his desire in the pursuit of the call of God became very evident.

He had held back for years in stepping forward for ministerial training because he knew well how such theological schools had killed the spirit of many. Prior to the revival, academic qualifications and learning came to be more emphasized for the ministry than a spiritual life and fervency.

Eventually he was recommended for the ministry by Moriah Chapel in 1903 which meant the trial of his preaching skills in Moriah and other associated chapels. It also meant that his personal experience with Christ and his call to the ministry would be scrutinised by mature godly men. It is of interest to note that George Muller's writings on faith and prayer had left quiet a mark upon him in his walk with God. In these days as he prepared for ministry he was praying much in faith that God would baptise him with the Holy Spirit.

He was no victim of higher-criticism or modernism but believed in the depravity of man's heart, the eternal punishment of Christ rejecters and of the miracle working power of God to save sinners through the atoning blood of Christ. He preached obedience, holiness and subjection to Christ. Initially he was deeply depressed over the state of the church generally as it was a sad failure in comparison to Scripture. But one night while trying to prevail with God in prayer and before breaking through, he fell asleep. In the middle of the night he awoke suddenly with unspeakable joy in the very presence of Almighty God. For four hours he spoke to the Lord face to face as a friend would. From that moment he knew God was going to work in the land. A similar burden of prayer came to him every night for the next 4 months. It would be wrong to say that this was the beginning of his prayer for revival for he had been praying for the previous 11 years that God would send revival to Wales and for 13 years for a personal filling of the Holy Spirit.

In September 1904 aged 26, he moved to Newcastle Grammar School for preliminary studies. It was here that he would have a meeting with God that would be as significant as Moses meeting God at the burning bush.

Seth Joshua, pioneer Evangelist for the Calvinistic Methodist Forward Movement, had been mightily converted back in 1882 at a Salvation Army meeting when he knelt at an old wooden seat and cried unto God for forgiveness and salvation. Those were days when Salvationists had invaded the valleys with a revival spirit. They held open-airs and the salvation lasses played their tambourines amidst testimonies and shouts of "hallelujah." The CM Forward Movement had been founded by denominational leaders as an aggressive attempt to reach the Welsh communities which were unmoved by the power of the Gospel. The Forward Movement certainly carried something of the spirit of those Salvationists and so did Seth.

Those who knew him called him a 'Man of God' for he was wholly dedicated and consecrated unto God. He was a man that God could use. He was not bound by typical trends of religion or tradition. For some time he had been greatly concerned about the emphasis on education rather than an emphasis on a real spiritual experience and walk with God as the singular qualification for ministry. He continued with a deep burden and prayer laid upon him by God that He would "...take a lad from the coal-mine or from the field, even as He took Elisha from the plough, to revive His work."

When Seth came to Newcastle Emlyn to hold a campaign, the Principal of Evan Roberts' school encouraged all the boys to attend the meetings. At these meetings Evan was much impressed with the fervour and message of the preacher as he sat night after night intently listening to this messenger from God. The campaign ended without any unusual manifestation or sign that God was about to do a great work. Seth Joshua thought the ground seemed hard and the people unresponsive. Even Evan found his own heart to be somewhat hard and cold. The Evangelist moved on to his next place, a small neighbourhood on the coast of Cardigan Bay, but there were some very definite workings of God in the hearts of the people. A group of the students from the Grammar School made plans to travel to these meetings with Evan among them.

As they travelled they sang "It is coming; it is coming; the power of the Holy Ghost. I receive it; I receive it; the power of the Holy Ghost." After the first early morning meeting Seth Joshua prayed asking God to "bend them". This prayer became Roberts' prayer in a powerful way. Now he prayed "bend me Lord" with all his heart. Soon this would become the prayer of a nation. In the next morning meeting young Evans fell upon his knees and then lay prostrate asking God this one thing "bend me, bend me". He was sweating profusely as he travailed in prayer and groaned in spirit. That day he died, he became a new man, another man. It was a virtual baptism of fire in which God did bend him. These meetings continued for several days with other young friends having similar experiences. Evan was now given over to prayer for a great spiritual awakening in Wales. It became impossible for him to carry on his studies. He asked God for others who were filled with fire who would stand by him in the task ahead, they were soon given to him. He made initial plans to step out in faith with this little band in evangelistic labourers from county to county but it seems the Lord restrained him from such.

During these weeks there were those looking on who felt Evan was losing touch with reality, becoming fanatical and extreme. They were very concerned about him. One of the nights Evan and Sidney were up in the middle of the night travailing in prayer for souls when their hostess came and rebuked them for the noise at such an unusual time.

It was in the Sunday morning meeting as Evan Phillips preached on "Father the hour is come" that Evan had a vision of the church in Louchor with young men sitting in rows and he was preaching to them. The Spirit of God was commissioning him to go and speak to them. Finally he yielded to God's will. After speaking with his Principal he left Newcastle Emlyn on the 31st of October for Louchor by train. All he had was the Holy Spirit. No one was expecting him in Louchor and no meetings were arranged. His family were sceptical of his enthusiasm and his minister slow to arrange a meeting but finally he persuaded the various older ministers in the area to allow him to speak at their churches that week. The first meeting was a youth meeting held on the Monday night. There were just seventeen present. As he testified of what God had been doing and was about to do he exhorted them to prepare themselves for a baptism of the Holy Ghost. At first the meeting was hard but finally the power of God came down and all who were not saved were instantly converted and the others yielded themselves unreservedly to God.

The next day news of the deep effect and change in the lives of these youth spread. Night after night meetings were held with more gathering in as he went from church to church. The people prayed, listened, repented and rejoiced. His message to sinners was repent, his message to the saints was be filled with the Spirit. By the end of the week the community was astir. Meetings went on for 5 hours, many lay prostrate on the ground under deep conviction of sin and agony of soul until they received salvation. The following week, meetings continued to 5 in the morning with sleep, food and normal activities forgotten.

Then an invitation came from a church in Aberdare where the proposed speaker had cancelled his Sunday morning engagement. Evan arrived there with three young ladies accompanying him. The congregation was trundling along in normalcy, but not for long. The church elders expected a good service but nothing unusual. The service began with one of the young ladies bursting into song as tears rolled down her cheeks. The young preacher was bent over in his seat shaking as he wept. Suddenly one of the church's proudest members fell on her knees and confessed her sins publicly in agonising prayer. People knelt everywhere. The organ remained silent and the service went on all day. By that nightfall the community was astir and a great host gathered at this chapel. Some were singing "O, the Lamb, the Bleeding Lamb" or "Throw out the lifeline, throw out the lifeline." Others were praying and travailing. Some were sitting, many were kneeling, and others were prostrate. Words of knowledge flowed from the young revivalist. Meetings continued, fire spread and homes were changed. The same thing happened in every chapel in this community that sought God.

The services were spontaneous and unorganised. People prayed, testified and sang as prompted by the Spirit of God. Reports began to appear in newspapers which at first were very disparaging but not long after when reporters were also converted, the papers carried very supportive reports. News of this Welsh Revival now spread abroad to many nations.

At times Evan could preach for hours, other times he gave short direct words (always in the Welsh language). Sometimes he cried, sometimes he laughed and rejoiced. He was of course most prominent; a vessel rose up by God to lead but the revival was everywhere. Many ministers arose to preach and lead their people back to God and into revival. **National sports were deserted; theatres were emptied; pubs closed and crime dropped. In Cardiff police reported that drunkenness dropped by 60% within one month of the revival beginning. This revival even invaded brothels and gambling dens. Hardened, cursing miners were suddenly transformed and they would have been regarded to be the hardest people to reach in the land.** Agnostics repented and put faith in the Blood of the Lamb for forgiveness. Children prayed down the power of God. At the centre of every prayer, song and the message were Calvary and the bleeding Lamb.

Preachers came from across Britain and the world to see the glory of the Lord fill His temple. When **F.B. Meyer**, the famous London preacher came to investigate this outpouring, he was urged to preach but refused and sat silent in the School of the Holy Ghost. **G. Campbell Morgan** scared of being a hindrance finished his preaching engagements and told Roberts he was leaving. When asked his opinion about the revival he said it is "Pentecost continued". **William Booth** packed his bag and left the revival as quickly as possible. These great preachers and leaders were scared to touch this work of God. They sat idly by while children and old coal miners waxed eloquent in prayer and testimony. True revival is never organised by man, committees or denominations. The fear of God amidst manifestations of righteousness protected the work. Roberts himself strove to keep out of sight and not to hinder God working. He refused to have photos taken of him and refused many international invitations to minister.

Even politicians had to take note. **Mr Lloyd George** a Member of Parliament (and later Prime minister of Britain) said "...it is certainly the most remarkable spiritual movement this generation has witnessed... It seems to be rocking Welsh life like a great earthquake."

This revival especially captured the youth but it never missed or neglected the old. It was a singing revival but the songs were crammed with sound doctrine. It was a time of blessing for the church but the emphasis was on seeing sinners saved. It was indeed a Welsh revival (not a British Revival) but the fire did carry across Britain, Europe and the world by those whose tongue was touched by a coal from of the altar. A desire and love for reading the scriptures resulted from this revival. Holiness of heart and conduct was wrought mightily. Worldly methods of drawing and keeping people in the church were nullified. This was a Heaven Sent Revival. One eye witness said "DIVINE MOVEMENTS have their birthplace in the heart of deity."

At a glance, what were the final results of this revival? Within 2 months of its beginnings there had been over 30,000 converts. Within six months 100,000 converts. By the beginning of 1906 who could know? By 1910 its influence was felt in every corner of the globe. Religious systems in Britain tried to explain it all away by claiming it was the product of Welsh emotion but for over 100 years it has been regarded as a major part of the Christian heritage and saints continue to be encouraged and challenged by it. Evan Roberts finally went to be with the Lord in January 1951.

Dearly beloved, this is the only time we can call ours in the history of this church. In another 50 years if Jesus tarries to come, most of us will no longer be here. Now that we have the unusual opportunity of being here, let us leave a legacy of revival for the coming generation. Let's give this course our best, for generations unborn to have a place of spiritual solace. May God give us some more spiritual madness and enthusiasm like Evan Roberts!

CHAPTER 3

WANTED! WANTED!! WANTED!!!

Mantle Carriers…

"And it came to pass, when the LORD was about to take Elijah into heaven by a whirlwind, that Elijah went with Elisha from Gilgal. Then Elijah said to Elisha, 'stay here, please, for the LORD has sent me on to Bethel." And Elisha said, 'As the LORD lives, and as your soul lives, I will not leave you!' So they went down to Bethel. And the sons of the prophets who were at Bethel came out to Elisha, and said to him, 'do you know that the Lord will take away your master from over you today?' And he said, 'Yes, I know; keep silent!' Then Elijah said to him, 'Elisha, stay here, please, for the LORD has sent me to Jericho.' And he said, 'As the LORD lives, and as your soul lives, I will not leave you!' So they went to Jericho. And the sons of the prophets who were at Jericho came to Elisha and said to him, 'Do you know that the LORD will take away your master from you today?' So he answered, 'Yes, I know; keep silent!' Then Elijah said to him, 'Stay here, please, for the LORD has sent me on to the Jordan.' And he said, 'As the LORD lives, and as your soul lives, I will not leave you!' So the two of them went on. And fifty men of the sons of the prophets went and stood facing them at a distance, while the two of them stood by the Jordan. Now Elijah took his mantle, rolled it up, and struck the water; and it was divided this way and that, so that the two of them crossed over on dry ground. And so it was, when they had crossed over, that Elijah said to Elisha, 'Ask! What may I do for you, before I am taken away from you?' And Elisha said, 'please let a double portion of your spirit be upon me.' So he said, 'You have asked a hard thing. Nevertheless, if you see me when I am taken from you, it shall be so for you; but if not, it shall not be so.' Then it happened, as they continued on and talked, that suddenly a chariot of fire appeared with horses of fire, and separated the two of the; and Elijah went up by a whirlwind into heaven. Now Elisha saw it, and he cried out, 'My father, my father, the chariot of Israel and its horsemen!' And he took hold of his own clothes and tore them into two pieces. He also took up the mantle of Elijah that had fallen from him, and went back and stood by the bank of the Jordan. Then he took the mantle of Elijah that had fallen from him, and struck the water, and said, 'Where is the Lord God of Elijah?' And when he also struck the water, it was divided this way and that; and Elisha crossed over. Now when the sons of the prophets who were from Jericho saw him, they said, 'The spirit of Elijah rests on Elisha.' And they came to meet him, and bowed to the ground before him." **2 Kings 2:1-15 (NKJV)**

"So I sought for a man among them who would make a wall, and stand in the gap before Me on behalf of the land, that I should not destroy it; but I found no one." **Ezekiel 22:30 (NKJV)**

From the above text in 2 Kings Chapter 2 verses 9, 13, 14 and mark the words **"MANTLE","MANTLE OF ELIJAH", "THE SPIRIT OF ELIJAH RESTS ON ELISHA."** Every office or position has a particular item to associate it with. For example, we associate a sceptre, crown, throne and staff with a king or queen.

A mantle is generally understood as a Garment, Veil, Blanket, Robe, Wraps, Shawl or Cloak (Hebrew-adderet, תרדא), suitable for travelling on foot in the hot sun and sleeping outside on cold desert nights

 But Scripturally and spiritually a mantle symbolizes a calling, ministry, sign of one chosen of God, the glory of God, the protection (covering) of God, and the authority given by God for a responsibility, anointing and office. In the ancient times of the Bible, the mantle was part of the official garment of a prophet. The mantle automatically marked a man as a prophet, a spokesman of God.

When mantle is bestowed on a man, it gives that man the supernatural ability to complete an assignment, task or commission. One of the many challenges facing the 21st century Christians and ministries is; mission without the mantle for that mission. A number of us have commissioned our ministries leaving behind the cloak for that ministry. Every ministry you see has a mantle. Sadly, some of us are already in the ministry without the mantle of the said ministry.

Mantle is something they put on you and you perform in accordance to the assignment given. Mantle is not handkerchief, anointed water or oil. Handkerchief, anointed water or oil is faith points of contact. Mantle is the totality of equipment given to a man to take an assignment-divine assignment.

Mantle does not just fall on anybody. It's not just because you are in the church that qualifies you to carry a man's mantle. You don't get a man's mantle by being his friend, relation or child. Mantle does not come by working in the same ministry. It does not come by sitting down and listening to a man preaches. We have seen and heard about great men of God rise and go and their mantles disappear from the earth; great ministries evaporate from the earth because there are no men to pick up these mantles.

God may have taken our fathers-these generals; He did not take the mantles with them. His challenge with us is this: there are no heads upon which these cloaks will rest upon or men and women that will pick up these mantles. **Wanted! Wanted!! Wanted!!! New Elisha's to pick up these cloaks. "So I sought for a man among them…"** As Elijah was taken up into heaven, he allowed his mantle—the symbol of his prophetic call—to fall down to the earth, and Elisha took it up. Elisha received Elijah's enduement, but that anointing was to fulfil Elijah's task. God's commission authority on Elijah remained even when he left. The Elijah's mantle was transferable. The mantle of Elijah-Elisha is still alive. The mantles of our fathers are still alive!

What made Elijah a great prophet and Elisha a great prophet was what made John the Baptist a great prophet too. The same Spirit which was upon Elijah made the Apostles what they were. Still, it didn't end there. The mantle and Spirit of Elijah and Elisha, of John, of the Apostles and of the early Church have never left. The men of the historic revival have passed away. All have gone but there remain those mantles that drove their ministries. The same thing, power, authority and Spirit that belong to the great men and women of God of the past are ours and what is ours belongs to them.

The same mantle that handed over Scotland to **John Knox** and also made Queen Mary said "I fear the prayer of John Knox more than the armies of Europe" is still alive.

Smith Wigglesworth was without doubt one of the most anointed men of God that has lived in the recent times. He was known as the Apostle of Faith. He lived and walked continually in the presence of God. And the miracles that accompanied his ministry were of the sort that has rarely been seen since the days of the Apostles. People born blind and deaf, cripples-twisted and deformed by disease, others on death's door with cancer or sickness of every kind, all were healed by the might power of God through this servant. Even the dead were raised. He lived in the very presence of God. The mantle that made him do all these and more is still alive.

The mantle of **George Whitefield**, history's greatest open air speaker, who preached to over 70,000 without a loud speaker, whose altar calls ranges up to 10,000, whose voice could be distinctly heard almost a mile away is still alive and available till today.

Jonathan Edwards's mantle for preaching salvation, even though he read his sermons (as was the custom of the day), people fell under the power of the Holy Spirit is still alive waiting for heads to rest on.

Charles Finney had a mantle for prayer and preaching. God used him to birth the Second Great Awakening. **Finney's** anointing–and the Presence that he carried–was so powerful that he would ride through towns without even getting off the train and revival would break out in those towns. He would walk into factories, and the workers would fall to their knees and confess their sins to God before **Finney** would say a word. **Finney** was so anointed with the Holy Spirit that people were often brought under conviction of sin just by looking at him. When holding meetings at Utica, New York, he visited a large factory there and was looking at the machinery. At the sight of him one of the operatives, and then another, and then another broke down and wept under a sense of their sins, and finally so many were sobbing and weeping that the machinery had to be stopped while **Finney** pointed them to Christ.

Sometimes the power of God was so manifest in his meetings that almost the entire audiences fell on their knees in prayer or were prostrated on the floor. When in the pulpit he sometimes felt almost lifted off his feet by the power of the Spirit of God. Some persons believe that the moral work of the Holy Spirit is not accompanied by any physical manifestations; but both in Bible times and in Finney's meetings remarkable physical manifestations seemed to accompany the moral work of the Holy Spirit when the moral work was deep and powerful. At times, when Finney was speaking, the power of the Spirit seemed to descend like a cloud of glory upon him. Often a hallowed calm, noticeable even to the unsaved, seemed to settle down upon cities where he was holding meetings. Sinners were often brought under conviction of sin almost as soon as they entered these cities. This mantle is still alive. Can someone like Elisha pick up this cloak?

Kathryn Kuhlman had a special relationship with the Holy Spirit. She carried a mantle for preaching the Word, with confirmation by the Holy Spirit through healings and miracles. That mantle is still alive.

Benson Idahosa is a man God mightily used to shake nations of the earth. He is gone but his cloak is still here and available. The Lord desires to do greater and mightier things in and through us. He longs for it. He wants it. He promised it and He is ready to do it. God wants to do even in greater measure what He did in and through this servant of His. He is available to pick up the cloak?

The anointing and authority God gave to **Oral Robert** did not leave when he departed. The same Spirit that was upon this great servant of God is still here. Let somebody reach out to take it.

Aimee Semple McPherson, God mightily used her to impact her time, Her services was known for divine healing, where repentant would walk without crutches, regain lost eyesight, heal broken bones, and leave their wheelchairs to walk. She made an amazing impact on her world as a preacher and servant of the Most High God. Guess what? Her legacy lives on!

Maria Woodworth-Etter was undoubtedly the most successful female evangelist of the early 20th Century. Her meetings were marked by the manifestations that many associated with frontier revivals of the early 19th Century, and her pulpit persona was commanding. "The power which was given to the apostles in their day had never been taken from the church. The trouble was, the churches had sunk to the level of the world and were without the unlimited faith that will heal the sick and make the lame to walk. She prayed for the return of the old days and more faith in Christ among the people." Woodworth Etter. Her mantle is still alive.

Evans Robert a great revivalist who pioneered a tremendous move of the Spirit of God in Wales. He is gone, his mantle is still alive.

A.W. Tozer carried a mantle for seeing God as He really is in the third Heaven, and communicating what he saw to earth. That cloak is still alive. Can someone reach out for it?

REQUIREMENTS FOR ANY MANTLE

Some have wishes, Others like the anointing on Elijah, Elisha, Moses, Joshua, John the Baptist, Paul, Peter, Billy Graham, John Knox, Apostle Joseph Ayo Babalola, John G. Lake, Kathryn Kuhlman, Morris Cerrulo, Benson Idahosa, Smith Wigglesworth, Billy Graham, Reinhard Bonnke, William Seymour, Elijah, Charles G. Finney, Rev Oral Roberts, Noah, Aimee Semple Mcpherson, John Wesley, Martin Luther, John Wycliffe, T. L. Osborn, Charles Spurgeon, Pa Josiah Akindayomi, Maria Woodworth-Etter, Charles Fox Parham and Evan Roberts.

We have seen and heard of people who wished to carry certain cloak or mantle of a certain great servant of God and died still wishing. Let me clear this; seed sowing does not guarantee you access to these mantles. Seed sowing can only guarantee you access to taping into someone's grace and anointing but not carrying the mantle. The need of the hour is mantle wearers, anointing carriers, people who will take up their mantle and never lay it down. There are more mantle's resting on the ground today than mantle's that have been picked up and worn.

We shall be considering factors that qualified Elisha to pick up Elijah's cloak or mantle and others in relation to what can qualify you and I to carry the mantle of a man you covet his ministry or grace. Stay with me as we explore these ancient secrets.

MANTLE IS A DNA THING

Understand this, God Determines our Mantle Ahead of Time. We do not select a mantle; it is established and destined by God. Elisha didn't just receive Elijah's mantle because he happened to be at the right place at the right time. It was already his according to God's word. **"Also anoint Jehu son of Nimshi king over Israel and anoint Elisha son of Shaphat from Abel Meholah to succeed you as prophet" 1 Kings 19:16.** Elisha only needed to collaborate with the call of God on his life to collect the mantle that was his by God's appointing. Elisha's hunger and pursuit of Elijah was a sign of what God had placed in his heart.

Joseph also knew at a very young age, through prophetic dreams, that God had called him to rule. A mantle is not ours for the choosing, it is determined ahead of time by God. The desire God places in our hearts is just one indication, among other confirmations, of the calling that is ours. Prophetically, I know the ministry I belong to. I know my DNA; I know the mantle family I belong to and I am following it with the whole of my being.

ON HAND MEN

Unfortunately some of us are not liable for the mantle of a man we covet to rest on simply because of unavailability. This availability does not in any way mean physical presence alone. You can carry the mantle of a man you are physically far away from but spiritually close to. **"And so it was, when they had crossed over, that Elijah said to Elisha, 'Ask! What may I do for you, before I am taken away from you?' And Elisha said, 'please let a double portion of your spirit be upon me.' So he said, 'You have asked a hard thing. Nevertheless, IF YOU SEE ME WHEN I AM TAKEN FROM YOU, IT SHALL BE SO FOR YOU; BUT IF NOT, IT SHALL NOT BE SO." 2 Kings 2:9-10.**

People wear someone's cloaks because they make themselves available. Mantle does not rest on a person because he is perfect or talented, rather because he sees the Spirit when it drops. Gehazi, no matter his closeness to Elisha did not qualify him to be the next Elisha or carry the mantle of Elisha. Instead he was struck with the leprosy of Naaman **(2 Kings 5:27)**. At a point, **"Elisha said to Gehazi, 'Tuck your cloak into your belt, take my staff in your hand and run. If you meet anyone, do not greet him, and if anyone greets you, do not answer. Lay my staff on the boy's face… Gehazi went on ahead and laid the staff on the boy's face, but there was no sound or response. So Gehazi went back to meet and told him, 'The boy has not awakened.'"** 2 Kings 4:29, 31.

What a disappointment! Even with Elisha, his staff and word, Gehazi could not perform. Why? Because he was bodily present but spiritually absent. Let's consider John the Baptist; he never saw Elijah or Elisha but he carried what these men carried. John was anointed with the same spirit and power which was upon Elijah. **"And he will go on before the Lord, in the spirit and power of Elijah, to turn the hearts of the fathers to their children and the disobedient to the wisdom of the righteous-to make ready a people prepared for the Lord."** Luke 1:17.

SERVICE POSITIONS YOU FOR YOUR MANTLE

For a long season, Elisha was a servant to Elijah, supporting him in a menial capacity and learning at his feet. **(2 Kings 3:11).** It can be tempting to go directly after a mantle, but just as with Elisha, God has established His timeline for your life. God positions you with people and leaders that He wants you to serve now. Serving with faithfulness and a teachable heart is a powerful means of being positioned to attain your God-ordained destiny.

BECOME A STUDENT TO THE CARRIER OF THE MANTLE YOU COVET

This works whether your spiritual father is alive or dead. He or she does not have to be alive in order for God to give you an impartation of the mantle your father carried. You place someone in the role of spiritual father when you honour him or her as an example and hero in your life. When you do that, you can ask God and He will give you an impartation from your father's life.

FOLLOW YOUR SPIRITUAL FATHER IN ALL GODLY WAY.

A son imitates his father. **Hebrews 13:7-9** instructs us to **"Remember those who rule over you, who have spoken the word of God to you, whose faith follow, considering the outcome of their conduct. Jesus Christ is the same yesterday, today, and forever. Do not be carried about with various and strange doctrines…."**

This passage is actually telling us to imitate our spiritual fathers, because the truths they taught us will not change. When we review the passage above in context, we see that the author was telling us: That what worked for our fathers will work for us. The truths our leaders taught us are still true for us. Because Christ doesn't change, neither does His doctrine. Therefore, we should not allow strange, new doctrines to carry us away from truth. We are to stick with the truths taught by our fathers; and we are to imitate our spiritual fathers in doctrine, faith, and conduct.

If you want to receive an impartation of what God has given your spiritual father, you need to live out this passage every day. For example: Listen intently as your father teaches, take the instruction to heart, and act on it. Notice the prayer life of your father and try to imitate it. Dig into the truths your father teaches you. Seek to understand those truths more clearly, so you can grow like your father has grown.

Emulating your father in every godly way changes you and honours your father. When you do that, God will honour you and bless you with more of the mantle your father carries.

BE RUGGEDLY PERSISTENT

"And it came about when the Lord was about to take up Elijah by a whirlwind to heaven, that Elijah went with Elisha from Gilgal. Elijah said to Elisha, "Stay here please, for the Lord has sent me as far as Bethel." But Elisha said, "As the Lord lives and as you yourself live, I will not leave you." So they went down to Bethel. Then the sons of the prophets who were at Bethel came out to Elisha and said to him, "Do you know that the Lord will take away your master from over you today?" And he said, "Yes, I know; be still." Elijah said to him, "Elisha, please stay here, for the Lord has sent me to Jericho." But he said, "As the Lord lives, and as you yourself live, I will not leave you." So they came to Jericho. The sons of the prophets who were at Jericho approached Elisha and said to him, "Do you know that the Lord will take away your master from over you today?" And he answered, "Yes, I know; be still." Then Elijah said to him, "Please stay here, for the Lord has sent me to the Jordan." And he said, "As the Lord lives, and as you yourself live, I will not leave you." So the two of them went on". (2 Kings 2:1-6).

We are told at the very beginning that these events took place when the Lord was about to take up Elijah by a whirlwind to heaven. By stating it in this way, the author has removed the suspense of what is going to happen to Elijah. That is already known. He does this because he wants us to focus on something else. He wants to direct our attention to Elisha.

These verses reflect Elisha's persistent commitment to Elijah. Their journey begins at Gilgal to Bethel, to Jericho, now to Jordan. Elijah to Elisha at all these locations remained behind. But Elisha would not quit. He was committed to staying with Elijah. What was the source of this commitment? I think that it was twofold. I think that there was a personal commitment to the man. But more importantly, Elisha was committed to the God of Elijah. This was primarily a SPIRITUAL commitment. Elisha was determined to partake of the same spiritual relationship that he had witnessed in the life of his teacher.

HONOUR YOUR FATHER-THE CARRIER OF YOUR MANTLE

The mantle a man carries cannot work for you without you submitting and honouring the authority of the mantle. Life flows through honour; mantles are released or flows through honour. There is a current of life, a continuity of power, blessings and supernatural release-that only comes to us when we actively honour our parents natural and spiritual respectively.

To honour someone means to esteem, recognition and respect toward another. To dishonour someone means to disdain, put down, belittle and insult. When you honour, esteem your father what your father carries will be transferred to you. The role of the carrier of your mantle is to train you up to be able to carry the mantle. Your father will nurture and protect you. Your father will pour out knowledge, understanding, wisdom, counsel and blessings. The role of your father is to make you successful in knowing the Lord and fulfilling the call of God on you.

DEAL WITH MONEY, MATERIAL AND FAME SEEKING TENDENCIES

This is the point at which many mantle seekers make shipwreck and their great works and desires come to an untimely end. The love of money on the part of some of us has done more to discredit our desire for mantle. Gehazi was meant to be the next to carry what left Elijah and rested on Elisha but because of love for money. **Love of money, fame and material things** denied him the privilege of carrying the mantle according to order. **"Gehazi, the servant of Elisha the man of God, said to himself, 'My master was too easy on Naaman, this Aramean, by not accepting from him what he brought. As surely as the LORD lives, I will run after him and get something from. So Gehazi hurried after Naaman. When Naaman saw him running toward him, he got down from the chariot to meet him. 'Is everything all right?' He asked. 'Everything is all right,' Gehazi answered. 'My master sent me to say, 'Two young men from the company of the prophets have just come to me from the hill country of Ephraim. Please give them a talent of silver and** two sets of clothing'…But Elisha said to him, 'Was not my spirit with you when the man got down from his chariot to meet you? Is this the time to take money, or to accept clothes, olive groves, vineyards, flocks, herds or menservants and maidservants?" 2 Kings 5:20, 21, 23, 26.

Loving money has cost some people their lives, ministry, lives of family members and of course their relationship with God. When you allow money becloud your visions, become your god, you will find out quickly that it makes a poor god. There is a tremendous difference between money and the love of money. A Christian can possess money but in a situation where money possesses a Christian makes it is dangerous.

WATCH YOUR MOTIVES

Why are you seeking for anointing, power, oil on your head? Why are you seeking for that grace? Inordinate intention is one of the major hindrances why the mantle has not rested on you yet. A number of us desire mantle to rest on us just for Selfish-for works of the flesh. The head of a self-centric-person cannot not pay host to a God-centric-mantle.To pick a mantle God designed for you, put your motives aright.

HUMBLE YOURSELF

Mantle does not and will never rest on an egotistical person. God refuses to accept the proud. God detests the proud. God counter the proud. **"God hates the proud but gives grace to the humble" James 4:6.** Humility is acknowledging and surrendering our ways to His ways. We need to absolutely depend on God, the same way babies depend on their parents.
If mantle rests on a proud brother or sister, all she does or he does will be through egocentric aspiration or vanity. If your purpose for asking for the cloak is for self-magnificence, fame, glory and showmanship; you can't have it. On the order hand, when this cloak is on a humble person all he does is to score points for God and to please God.

DEAL WITH THE SPIRIT OF ABSALOM (ABSALUM)

The spirit of Absalom is very similar to the spirit of Korah because it's also a spirit of rebellion. The spirit of Absalom echoes pride, disobedience, self-promotion and rebellion. Elisha was Elijah's attendant and servant. His time with Elijah was not only an education in theology and in practical ministry to others, but in humility, submission to authority, loyalty, faithfulness, and obedience in being a servant. All of this was vital to his training and preparation for ministry. In order to lead, one must first learn how to be led. In order to give directions, one must first learn how to receive and follow directions. In order to be faithful, one must first learn faithfulness.

PAY ATTENTION TO KNOW WHEN TO CASH IN
2 Kings 2:10 He said, "You have asked a hard thing. Nevertheless, if you see me when I am taken from you, it shall be so for you; but if not, it shall not be so."

Paying focused seems to be one of the most difficult things a human can do! Elijah's statement 'You have asked a hard thing', makes me wonder if he actually meant receiving the mantle or paying focused! Some say that the average attention span can vary from 20 minutes to just 8 seconds. We live in a restless world and in a struggle to survive or for some unknown cause our minds wander from one thing to another in a matter of seconds. Elijah tells Elisha that if he wanted to receive the double portion he needed to have his eyes on his master.

How can we look unto or stay focused on an unseen God? It is truly difficult in a world of attractions and distractions to stay focused on God since we do not see him through our fleshly eyes. So how do we focus on someone whom we are unable to see? The only way is to see Him is in our spiritual eyes.

CHAPTER 4

SET US ON FIRE OH LORD!

The greatest need of the church today is a mighty manifestation of the Spirit of God in revival power and fire. The most desperate need of the hour is a fresh Divine visit to impart a fresh vision of His glory, fresh fire, grace and simultaneously to reveal man's sinfulness and inadequacy. The words of Jesus in the Gospel of Luke chapter 12 verse 49, **"I have come to set the earth on fire, and how I wish it were already blazing!"**

Whenever the fire of God is released or sent, there is always a total transformation and complete change of life. But for it to happen, there must be burning desire for it. To light the fire of God in our present day church and society, our ablaze wish for this fire should be backed up with actions. Desire, longing, craving and aspirations remain a hallucination and daydream until it is put into action. The church (the body of Christ) has a power—whatever she agrees to do is attainable. If there is anytime we need to review our church vision and programs it is now.

If our craving in the church do not include zealousness for spiritual renewal and resurgence something is wrong somewhere. Now is the time to be deep concerned about the heart and spiritual life of everybody in the church, it's time to declare war against the works of the flesh, it's time to interest in the heart of our people the need for rebirth and renewal by the Holy Spirit, now is the time each and every one of us should deal with leftovers or bits and pieces of carnality in us if we must see and be part of the coming fire rain.

The results of the Lord setting us on fire are equally spectacular. The normal traits of ungodliness disappear. Blasphemy, filthy language, drunkenness and immorality. Tribalism, division and sentiments, dishonesty and selfishness are all replaced by a sweet sense of righteousness, peace and joy in the Holy Spirit. Sometimes entire towns or areas are affected. At other times whole nations are so blanketed with God's renewing activity that hardly any inhabited places are without some evidence of His glorious workings.

There are three kind of baptism mentioned in the gospel according to Matthew 3:11, "I indeed **baptized with water unto repentance:** but he that cometh after me is mightier than I, whose shoes I am not worthy to bear: he shall **baptize you with the Holy Ghost, and with fire.**" The baptism with water, the baptism with the Holy Spirit and the baptism of fire!

The baptism with water is an outward demonstration of our decision to give our lives to Christ and die to sin and worldly passions and affections, get buried in water and rise not unto the old nature and sinful lifestyle, but unto righteousness.

The baptism with the Holy Spirit is to dip us supernaturally into the belly of the sea of the Spirit, where we are immersed and filled, not with water, but with the Holy Spirit. In this state, it is much easier to operate and function in the Spirit. We are endued or armed with supernatural power to do so many things we could not do before now. At this point, we are more accessible to the Holy Spirit to relate to and work with us. Many of us have gone through church water baptism and experienced Holy Spirit baptism as well, but there is yet another Spirit baptism that we all need. The baptism of fire!

The baptism of fire, when it comes on a believer, it makes the believer very passionate for God and too hot for the devil. This fire brings drive, zeal, push and the driving force that makes a believer unstoppable. Thank God for water baptism and the Holy Ghost but we need some fire. All that God needed was only 120 men baptized with the Holy Ghost and fire and He took the whole world. Set us on fire oh Lord!

What is Fire?
Fire is one of the most powerful symbols, which represents God, His presence, His judgement and demonstrations. Fire here has to do with intensity of passion. When you say someone is on fire, it means the person is passionate about what he is doing or does. It means he is blazing and shining for God. Fire depicts the fiery holiness and fiery zeal the Holy Spirit kindles. Fire also refers to the judgment awaiting those who refuse the merciful ministry of the Spirit.

We need this fire at any cost, for only the fire of the Spirit can empower us to be victorious over the raging flames of hell that threaten the world and the church. Three things that is essential for abundant and victorious life. The Holy Spirit supplies these three essentials that we want to look at. If you quench the Spirit you will know it by weakness and defects in these three areas. First of all, fire is essential for- Heat, Light and Power.

HEAT

Take away the fire of the sun and earth becomes a giant iceberg. Life cannot survive without fire and the warmth it produces. This is true in the spiritual life also. Take away the fire of the Spirit and God's people will become God's frozen people. Instead of being a volcanic mountain the church becomes a snow-capped mountain. Give us a militant spirit, Lord. Come, set our spirit on fire. Give us a passion to share thy Word; give us consuming desire. Give us a flaming and burning zeal. Moving us forward and on. Help us the urgency, Lord, to feel. Till greater victory is won.

Early Christianity succeeded by the contagion of an enthusiasm." This is just another way of saying that they let the fire burn. They did not quench the Spirit, but let the heat of love warm their own hearts so that others could be warmed. If this heat is no present in our lives then we are quenching the Spirit.

LIGHT

Take away the light and man is blind to all beauty and truth. Take away the fire and spirit and man is left in the darkness of ignorance and shut off from the truth of God. As he refers to the emotional nature, so light refers to the intellectual nature of man. The fire of the Holy Spirit is essential for the head as well as the heart.

God forbid that any of us should be content to be cold and indifferent while the fires of hell are busy burning. Only the fire of the Spirit can defeat those demonic flames. Set us afire, Lord, stir us, we pray!

POWER

Fire the source of most of the power that made man what he is. Man is the animal that has made friends with fire said Henry Van Dyke. Atomic power is fire power. The power that takes astronauts into space is fire power. The source of power for most industry is fire power. Fire is power and that is why the Holy Spirit, who is referred to nearly 300 times in the New Testament alone, is constantly associated with power. The fire power of the Christian is dependent upon his being filled with the Spirit. Heat and light are forms of power, but they are ineffective if there is not enough power to move the will.

We need fire of sufficient power to do more than warm our own hearts and open our own eyes to truth. We need fire that is contagious, and fire that will move us to labours of love, and which will cause others to be kindled and become torches of testimony for the glory of God. "Let your light so shine before men that they may see your good works and glorify your

Father in heaven." If the fire of the Spirit is burning in us we will be empowered to do work that captures attention and admiration. If we tend to be lazy and uninvolved in labours for the church and the cause of Christ it is obvious we are quenching the Spirit. The Spirit is power, and so if we say that we are too tired to labour for Christ then we are quenching the Spirit.

In some quarters, God's design has been thrown out - man's design has been taken in. The church of today is gradually shifting from the church God established in Acts. Today, man sets the rules, man determines what is right and what is not, man determines what he will allow God to do and not do. We are no longer the Church - we simply go through the motions of playing church. The church-world has become a dark wilderness -the Gospel message is diluted in some quarters; true repentance is overlooked; total transformation has become a rarity; preachers, pastors and teachers rarely speak about sin, judgment, and hell - these are now big no-no's. Light a fire, Lord! Burn away the crude; burn away the hardness; burn away the immorality; burn away religion; burn away anything that hinders! Until we as the true Church get tired of playing church.

The tragedy of the present day church is that we have too many dead and cold men from pulpit to pew. When Jesus walked the surface of the earth, nobody who had an encounter with the Master remained the same. Lives were changed as a result of the encounter with the Master. When the disciples carried their 'thus saith the Lord' message to the utmost parts of the world, lives were transformed and societies were turned upside down as evidenced in the book of Acts of the Apostles. For God to set us on fire in our present day church and society there must be very strong yearning for it; from all sundry; leadership to the followership. We need desperately spiritual arousing from our current state of spiritual comatose, dormancy, deadness or stagnation in our lives as believers and church.

There is a strange thing I have seen with this present day church and Christianity; it is preaching and doing God's work without fire. Preaching with the fire kills instead of giving life. The fire-less preacher is a savour of death unto death. The Word is not penetrating or does not live unless the fire is upon the preacher. In all our getting my generation-let's get fire.

Carrying fire cannot be learned, only earned by prayer. Fire is God ranks on a soldier preacher or Christian who has wrestled in prayer and gained the victory. Fire is like dynamite.

WHEN HE SENDS THE FIRE

Today's church needs a good dose of Holy Ghost fire! If there's anything that catches people's attention and causes them to sit up and take notice of what we are saying or doing, it's fire of the Holy Ghost. Someone once asked a great man of God what the secret of his success was and he replied, "I just get on fire for God and the World comes out to see me burn!" But if you haven't got the fire, if your Christianity is nothing but cold dead container-no warmth, no heat-you will never inspire anyone to do anything! He who has no fire in himself cannot warm others.

That's what's wrong with most of the churches today: Materialism, they have seemingly got everything. But they are one colossal failure because they have lost the SPIRIT and the FIRE!--No anointing or power, no real emotion, no dramatic charisma!--Their fire has gone out and they are dead as a doornail!

What good is a furnace when its fire goes out? It's cold and dark and useless! But it's still all there--just no fire. In some countries, if the furnace goes dead, cold and dark, the whole house will grow freezing cold.--And, heartbreaking to say, that is what is happened to most of the churches. Their pastors, preachers, prophets and leaders have lost their fire; they have no emotion, no spirit, no anointing, and no power. The fire's gone out, so the whole house has grown cold and frozen in lifeless, Spiritless, religion, human tradition, modus operandi, formulas, operations, formalities and procedures!

If we are on fire, the World will come out to watch us burn! But if we are dead, lifeless and cold, we will never attract or draw anyone to our message about the Lord and His Love! If we are not on FIRE, it doesn't matter how "good" a witness we may be, how many Bible verses we can quote, if we are not on FIRE, it's just cold-dead-facts and figures--no warmth, no heat, no life! We will never set anybody else on fire. All we will do is get them messed up and turned off.

Let's face it, as Christians, what are we here for?--To witness the Lord's Love and Truth to others!--And to really witness you have got to turn it on, to "let your LIGHT so SHINE before men!"--Matthew 5:16. You have got to be ALIVE, WHOLE-HEARTED and fired up to be able to show others that what you have with JESUS is BETTER than what they have without Him! Even if it's only one person you are witnessing to, you have got an audience and you have got to be ALIVE and on fire. People will judge the LORD by what they see and hear in YOUR witness to them!--Of course, witnessing is not merely "performing", putting on a show or pretending.--

When you're witnessing, you are enacting and trying to show others the TRUTH!--But if you're just talking theology and droning on about the Bible, quoting verses like a lot of church people do--blah blahblah like it's nothing but empty words or nursery rhymes-you are not going to win anyone. Quote me!

The words the Scribes and the Pharisees spoke were well-educated, but they were dry and dead and only brought death! Why?--Because they only spoke from their heads. But JESUS spoke from His HEART, from the SPIRIT, and it brought LIFE and MOVED people, not just tickling their ears, but reaching and touching their HEARTS! He said, "The WORDS that I speak, they are SPIRIT and they are LIFE!"--John 6:63.--THAT'S the DIFFERENCE!

Here are few things that happen when He sends the fire:

WE WILL NO LONGER BE "FORMS OF GODLINESS"

If the fire refuses to come we will be best religious bigots. We go to church, sing the right songs, speak in a Christian vocabulary yet nothing serious changed or happened in our lives. We arrive sick we go home sick. We met sick ones we leave them sick too. We bring problems from our marriages and homes we leave with them. With this some people are discouraged about our faith and they go back to their old ways and human mechanism to deal with life problems and challenges.

When all these happen it means the church and true essence of Christianity is missing. **2 Timothy 3:5 "having the form of godliness but denying its power"** church, it is this fire that really reveal our real essence. Set us on fire again!

WE WILL WITNESS WITH HIS POWER

When we are baptized with Holy Ghost and fire, we will witness Jesus to our generation with fire and in power. What a barren life it is when doing ministry without the baptism with Holy Ghost and the fire. Sometimes, committee and church leaders sends people to missionary field armed them with knowledge, all human and material resources but completely failed to arm them with Holy Ghost and Fire. Jesus sent out His disciples with Power and Fire, the same we had. But today, we do things our own way, imploring logic and human ideologies to supernatural business. No wonder we are barren spiritually. Doing spiritual things in with human logic, ideology and ways leads to spiritual barrenness. God's things must be done in His way only. Holy things must be done in holy ways only. Holy Ghost and fire things must be done in Holy Ghost and fire way.

THE CHURCH WILL STOP BEING A DEN OF THIEVES AND BECOME THE HOUSE OF PRAYER

Today, we see thieves in some quarters inform of Pastors, Bishops, Evangelists, Ministers, Prophets, Apostles, Deacons and what have you. Should this fire come, they will be raked out of the sanctuary. "Jesus entered the temple area and drove out all who were buying and selling there. He overturned the tables of the money changers and the benches of those selling doves. It is written, He said to them, My house will be called a house of prayer, but you are making it a den of robbers" Matthew 21:12-13. Had Jesus-the Fire did not show up at that time, buying and selling in the sanctuary would have been normal. Criminals, armed robbers on pulpits and rascals among us will no longer be comfortable should this fire come.

THE CHURCH WILL STOP BEING A HOUSE OF MEN AND BECOME THE HOUSE OF GOD

In the house of men human activities operates but no spiritual or supernatural activity; there is no miracles and signs, there is no deliverance, there is no transformation or change in heart. There is no life of God in the house of men! There are churches and ministries that have great attendance and membership, with lots of activities but God is not with them. Should this fire shows up, the will be life. The house of God is a house of life. The Spirit moves and demons are cast out, dead raised back to life, sickness healed, lives and marriages are changed. How we longed for this restoration of this house.

THE CHURCH WILL CEASE FROM BEING AN ENTERTAINMENT CENTRE TO SPIRITUAL CENTRE

Churches were the fire is lacking, praise and worship becomes nothing more than a concert. Likewise sermons become motivational messages that lack the power and tenacity to make or lead people to grow in faith and spiritual maturity. When the Fire is around, there is no room for entertainment and flesh. Without this Holy Ghost and Fire, we are nothing more than entertainers. Without the Holy Ghost and Fire the church is nothing more than an entertainment centre.

IF WE MUST CARRY THIS FIRE

Be hungry and thirsty for God
"On the last and greatest day of the feast, Jesus stood and said in a loud voice, if anyone is thirsty, let him come to me and drink." John 7:37. Hunger and thirst come before eating and drinking. The Lord will not

fill anyone that does not hunger and thirsty for Him. If you are not hungry for the Holy Ghost and Fire forget it, it won't come on you. Hunger for God and His Fire makes one go after God in order to know Him and receive more of Him. Anyone desiring the rain of fire on his life and ministry must feel, I need the Holy Ghost and this Fire and mean it so deeply and strongly that you depend solely on Him. Hunger makes one go for God beyond the normal realm. If you can't seek God beyond your convenient and comfort forget this fire-grace not withstanding! Fire does not come on anyone that is hunger less and thirsty less.

God cannot take you beyond the level of your contentment. If you are ok at the level where you are now, you will not receive more. Without hunger for God, you will not leave where you are to where you ought to be.

Deny yourself
Why are you praying for anointing, power, oil on your head, grace and fire of the Holy Ghost? Self is one of the major hindrances why He has not sent the fire yet. Self is one of the works of the flesh. Flesh cannot not pay host to this Fire. Here is the confession of a man longing the rain of fire: **"I have been crucified with Christ and I no longer live but Christ lives in me. The life I live in the body, I live by faith in the son of God who loved me and gave Himself for me" Galatians 2:20**. To carry this fire, the flesh-self need to be put where it belong. Self is pride, jealousy, strive, division, stubbornness, envy, deception and lust. Self cannot dethrone flesh and flesh cannot dethrone self. A proud and self-centred individual cannot carry this fire.

To carry this Fire requires death and that death is saying no to 'Dr Self' this Dr Self has the capacity of unseating God in the life of a man. Denying self means renouncing your personal egoism, ambitions, opinions, comfort, interest and pleasure. There is no shortcut to carrying this fire other than saying no to Mr Self.

Humble yourself
This fire does not and will never rest on an arrogant person. God resist the proud. God abhors the proud. God opposes the proud. **"God hates the proud but gives grace to the humble" James 4:6.** Humility is acknowledging and surrendering our ways to His ways. We need to absolutely depend on God, the same way babies depend on their parents.

If this fire rests on a proud brother or sister, all she does or he does will be through selfish ambition or conceit. If your purpose for asking for the fire of the Holy Ghost is for self-glory and showmanship; you can't have it. On the order hand, when this fire is on a humble person all he does is to score points for God and to please God.

Give yourself to a life of constant prayer

Another key to determine if we must carry this fire is life of constant prayer and communion with God. Prayer generates power, fire, flaming revival and supernatural results. A major cause of fire-less-ness and power-less-ness is prayer-less-ness. **"After they prayed, the place where they were meeting was shaking. And they were all filled with the Holy Spirit and spoke the word of God boldly." Acts 4: 31. "They saw what seemed to be tongues of fire that separated and came rest on each of them. All of them were filled with the Holy Spirit and began to speak in other tongues as the Spirit enabled them" Acts 2:3-4.**

Unfortunately today, prayer fire seems to be dying among us God's people, that is why we are dry and fire-less. If we must burn or aflame for Him prayer must not be neglected. One of the powers that God does not resist and will not resist is the power of prayer.

HOW TO KEEP THE FIRE BURNING IN YOUR LIFE
Leviticus 6:12; "Meanwhile, the fire on the altar must be kept burning; it must never go out."

So many who started on fire for God do not remain with the same fervency they once had. Today, a prevailing sin among us is the sin of lukewarmness that Jesus reprimanded us about. **"I know your works, that you are neither cold nor hot: I could wish were cold or hot. So then because you are lukewarm, and neither cold nor hot, I will spew you out of my mouth." Revelation 3:16.** Too often for too many of us, our spiritual temperatures change. We get on fire for God by attending of a revival meeting and rededicate our hearts only for a little later to be right back to being lukewarm and lackadaisical Christians again. You need to keep the fire on the altar of your heart on and red hot all the time. Lukewarmness is rampant in the church today? How can we recognize lukewarmness in our lives? Lukewarmness is manifested as a careless attitude towards the things of God. While there may be more, allow me to reveal few manifestations of lukewarmness.

Careless attitude toward the Scriptures
Appetite is a great sign of health. When there is no hunger to read and know the Word like you used to then lukewarmness has crept into your life. Usually you will notice people who are no longer on fire for God do not have time for the Scriptures. They have lost their passion for the Word. The

Psalmist says, 'My heart grew hot within me, and as I was meditated the fire burned then I spoke with my tongues' Psalm 39:3. The Word is the fire in the boiler room of your heart. Stay with the Word; go to a church that preaches the Word- the uncompromising Word.

Careless attitude towards prayer
No zeal for a powerful prayer life. You go to church but your prayer life is virtually nonexistent.

Prayer is to a believer is what Oxygen is to the body. To pray is to live and not to pray is to die. No one can really fulfil all that God designed for him without persistent and prevailing prayers. The men who have done the most for God in this world have been early on their knees. Through prayers Christians control the government of their nation. Revival is ignited by prayer and is sustained by it. If Jesus could not do without prayer, the present day Christians cannot do without it also. Look at what happen when you are prayerful;

Signs and wonders happens in your life on a frequent bases.
    You live a consistent victorious life
    You present the gospel with power
    You produce great result
    You dominate Cities
    You decide seasons and histories
    You control the spiritual
    You operate supernaturally
    With prayer the world is in your palms
    And so many other benefits

You must learn to wait on the Lord
Waiting is not wasting. It is very important we learn to wait on the Lord for sustenance of what we receive from the Lord. This is one important area of life the early men that interests me most. We are too in a hurry in this generation. Wanting everything done now now and quick quick. "On one occasion, while he was eating with them, he gave them this command: do not leave Jerusalem, but wait for the gift my Father promised, which you have heard me speak about." Acts 1:4. To wait on the Lord is waiting for God's time. Waiting upon the Lord is waiting in prayer and fasting. It means we need to spend more powerful time in God's presence.

Careless attitude towards Sanctification
What you would have never partook of years ago has become acceptable in your eyes all in the name of so called maturity and grace. It has made you

indifferent about personal holiness. The Word is no longer the alpha and omega in your life but society now determines what you believe is right or wrong.

Careless attitude towards Soul-winning

The Great Commission which is the only reason why Jesus left us here for is no longer your heartbeat. The Great Commission is now the greatest omission in your life. You cannot remember the last time you led somebody to Christ. Soul-winning is no longer a passionate pursuit.

Careless attitude towards Service

Your excuse, 'The church has hurt me', and that's why you are not involved in the local church. I'm going to be blunt with you, 'Who cares if the church hurt you? Did Jesus hurt you?' No! Then your excuse is not valid. The notion of sitting in church and do nothing is an indication that the fire has died on the altar. I won't go to church again! Who care? My pastor offended me. The elders and workers insulted me. They offended and insulted you but did Jesus offended and insulted you? That you stopped going to church because of a mere man is a sign that there is no fire burning in you at all. Get on fired my brother.

WAYS TO SUSTAIN AN IGNITED FIRE

Here are few outlined ways that will help you and I keep the fire of God in us burning:

Feed the Fire with the Word of God

Jesus said that man shall not live by bread alone but by every word that proceeds from the mouth of God. **Matthew 4:4**. Now I am not talking about dutifully doing your daily devotion with sleep filled eyes every morning. I am talking about hungrily searching the scriptures for the voice of the Lord within their pages. Revising and meditating on the word page by page, precept by precept and line by line to know the current saying of the Lord. This call demand we dig, till and plough into the scriptures and allow the Lord to start explaining the scriptures to you as well.

Fuel the Furnace with Prayer

There are three things you need to have a blazing fire and they are fuel, oxygen and heat. Prayer is the oxygen you use to stoke the flames high. Spending time in prayer is spending time in the presence of God, and the presence of God is the air that our souls need to be on fire. When you pray, you are breathing. You are taking in the vital element that gives life to your soul. "Prayer is the vital breath of the Christian; not the thing that makes him alive, but the evidence that he is alive." Oswald Chambers. When you pray, you are breathing. You are taking in the vital element that gives life to your soul.

Allow the Holy Spirit to Move

The Apostle Paul gives us a very pointed exhortation in **1 Thessalonians 5:19**. Do not suffocate the Holy Spirit. Is there anything in your life that is hindering the Spirit's work? Are you resisting doing something or giving up something that you know the Spirit is tapping you on the shoulder about? Do you have mindsets or mentalities that are contrary to allowing the Holy Spirit to move? If we must experience great breakthroughs spiritually we must stop telling the Holy Spirit how He can operate. We are very good at setting up preconditions that the Holy Spirit has to fulfil before we will believe that it is Him. We may be good at setting those preconditions up, but we should understand that the Holy Spirit will in most cases want to jump those conditions to establish what is better, bigger to those our conditions. Often those preconditions were limits the move of the Holy Spirit.

Do a Spring Clean-up Of Your Heart

The Bible says that in the last days the love of many will grow cold. Many times this is caused by unforgiveness and bitterness taking hold and growing in our hearts rather than love. We need to take time to do a spring clean-up of our heart and let go of any unforgiveness we may hold towards someone and remove any roots of bitterness that might have sprung up. Nothing puts out the flame of God's love faster than bitterness. Don't allow unforgiveness to freeze your soul. Guard your heart and deal with offenses quickly.

Start Making Your Fire Useful

Spiritual passion is ignited when it is being used to serve others. Start using the gifts and talents that God has given you to help others. Every believer in Jesus has been given gifts and talents and you are no exception. We must face our fears and stretch our faith as we begin to step out, but soon we will find there is no greater joy than being an instrument of the Holy Spirit to bless people. When we become obedient to stop burying our gifts and talents and start investing them into the lives of others, then we will be given even more to give. Matthew 25:14.

Spread the Flame

The major thing you can do to raise your spiritual hotness and light the fire of God in your life is to spread your flame. Just as John Wesley said that if you light yourself on fire that men will come from miles to watch you burn. Challenge yourself as you are reading this book to speak of your faith, share your testimony, and pray with people who need the reality of Jesus in their life.

EPILOGUE
GREATER WORKS THAN THESE…

"Most assuredly, I say to you, he who believes in Me, the works that I do he will do also; and greater works than these he will do, because I go to My Father." John 14:12-12

The Azusa Street Revival was catalytic and played a significant part in the expansion of the Pentecostal movement around the world. This revival may not be compared to what is about coming. The John Knox's, the Apostle Joseph Ayo Babalola's, the John G. Lake's, the Kathryn Kuhlman's, the Benson Idahosa's, the Smith Wigglesworth's, the Stephen's, the Moody's, the William Seymour's, the Elijah's, the Charles G. Finney's, the Oral Roberts's, the Noah's, the Aimee SempleMcpherson's, the John Wesley's, the Martin Luther, the John Wycliffe's, the T. L. Osborn's, the Charles Spurgeon's, Pa Josiah Akindayomi, Maria Woodworth-Etter, Parham, Charles Fox, Evan Roberts and so on, may have been mightily used by God in their respective times. I perceive in my spirit that major world shakers are emerging.

A man like Saint Patrick of Ireland born sometime around the year 385 in Scotland was so anointed by God that before the end of his life there were at least 33 interesting resurrection stories recorded. These resurrection stories include the raising up from the dead men and women, children, brothers and sisters, princes and princesses and not only that he raised dead people back to life; he also brought a dead horse back to life. At one point in his life he is said to have healed and brought back to life several mad cows owned by his aunt. Greater works than these shall you do…

Our Lord Jesus, performed many miracles while he was here on earth, demonstrating his power over nature and spirits. Our Lord **changed water into wine, Healed Peter's mother-in-law, Healed a leper, healed a centurion's servant, Raised a widow's son, Calmed the raging storm, Healed a woman with internal bleeding, He Raised Jairus' daughter, Healed blind men, Fed 5000 men and their families, Walked on water, Fed the 4,000 men and their families, used a fish as a bank, Raised of Lazarus from the dead** and many more others he did. Then he turned to his disciples and said "Most assuredly, I say to you, he who believes in Me, the works that I do he will do also; and greater works than these he will do…"

When we think about miracles in the New Testament, we often consider the miracles of Christ in the Gospel accounts. There are, however, many miracles recorded in the book of Acts. Let's take a little catch of these miraculous works. In Acts, Peter raised the disciple Tabitha from the dead, prison gate was miraculously opened (12:10). Paul blinded Elymus (13:11-12). Paul performed miracles in Iconium (14:3, 4). At Lystra, Paul healed a crippled man (14:8-18). Paul healed a woman possessed by an evil spirit (16:18). The miraculous earthquake unloosed all the chains and doors in the Philippians prison (16:26). Paul performed other miracles in Ephesus (19:11, 12). In Troas, Paul raised Eutychus from the dead (20:8-12). Paul was not affected by the viper at Melita (28:3-6). He also healed those on the island who were diseased (28:8-9). Peter heals the lame man at the Temple gate, Philip was snatched by the Spirit of the Lord to Azotos, Prison doors open for the Apostles, Peter liberated from prison by an angel, Chains fall from Paul and Silas, Ananias healed Saul's blindness (9:17-18). Peter healed Aeneas (9:32-35). In Joppa, Peter raised Dorcas from the dead (9:39-42). These acts did not stop with them. Greater works than these shall the ordinary hands of you and I do if we are ready!

"Behold, I will send you Elijah the prophet before the coming of the great and dreadful day of the LORD: and he shall turn the heart of the fathers to the children, and the heart of the children to their fathers, lest I come and smite the earth with a curse." **Malachi 4:5–6.** In this era, just prior to the second coming of Christ in the clouds of heaven. There will be the like of Elijah the prophet that will appear during this our time of political tyranny, dictatorship and great wickedness from the leadership of nations.

Take a look at the current administration and even what may be coming down the road; we can see a scary pattern taking place. Elijah in his time was marked to confront the powers that be and bring the nation back to the living God! Some churches in Nigeria are now full of entertainment, dead sermons and complacent saints operating in no power or apostolic anointing. Our churches are getting bigger and bigger while the signs and wonders are diminishing quickly, like apostle Paul 2 Timothy 3:5, churches would have a form of godliness but deny the power thereof and from such turn away.

This last-days Elijah generation is going to rise in the midst of this great spiritual drought and prepare the way of the Lord with an uncompromising message of repentance followed by demonstration and power! They will declare with authority "the Lord says" to the nation that has turned its back on God.

Today we see a great attack on the modern-day prophets and people of God who speak anything negative or deemed to be offensive. Ministers are now told not to preach on hell, repentance and even sin because it will turn members away from the church, resulting fear and intimidation to ministers of the gospel to preach the gospel with fire and conviction. But this last-days an army of God is raising up that will preach as Elijah and John the Baptist, with fire and conviction, with "thus saith the Lord!" and will not be concerned with the consequences it may have.

Ungodliness, violence, crime, economic difficulties, wars and so on in the world today is on increasing rate. In our nation today, the Church has become generally worldly and lukewarm in its love for Christ and is in great need of hearing and acknowledging the wake up calls. False religions are increasing all around us and get stronger year on year along.

What we need today in the world is a mighty manifestation of the glory of God in revival Power and Fire with signs following! In the Welsh revival of 1905 the nation was changed in a matter of weeks. Thousands upon thousands of unsaved people were, in a short time, moved by a heavenly influence to get right with God. The public houses and places of leisure were almost emptied and work areas were ablaze with talk about salvation; the old hymns were sung on the way to, and down the mines and new ones were composed; the churches over-flowed with the unconverted wanting to get saved from God's coming judgement on the world for its sin and rejection of his Son Jesus Christ. Greater works than these…

Don't wait any longer! This epistle is for you. The content and message in the book is for you. Don't wait till tomorrow, now is the long awaited time to respond to God. Allow the Holy Spirit to spark your life with the match of faith. Allow Him access your life to fulfil His agenda in the now through you.

Greater works than these… Lord, do it again!
Maranatha!

REFERENCE

An Account of the Life of John Wesley: Book of Martyrs Chapter 20 **Edited by William Byron**

Bahr, Robert. Least of All Saints: The Story of Aimee Semple McPherson. Englewood Cliffs, NJ: Prentice-Hall, 1979.

Bosworth, Fred F. "Pentecostal Outpouring in Dallas, Texas." Latter Rain Evangel, 10 July 1912.

Donald Gee, 'These Men I Knew' 1965; C. M. Robeck, Jr., art. 'International Dictionary of

Pentecostal and Charismatic Movements' 2002.

Epstein, Daniel Mark. Sister Aimee: The Life of Aimee Semple McPherson. New York: Harcourt, Brace, Jovanovich, 1993.

Frank Bartleman, Azusa Street (South Plainfield, N.J.: Bridge Publishing, 1980)

Bottom of Form

Gary B. McGee, "Parham, Charles Fox," in Biographical Dictionary of Christian Missions,

Gerald H. Anderson (New York: Macmillan Reference USA, 1998)

Gbile Akanni, What God looks for in His vessels (Nigeria: Peace House Publication, 1999.)

Christ for all Nations - Christ for all Nations. Retrieved 5 August 2017.

Goff, James R. Fields White unto Harvest: Charles F. Parham and the Missionary Origins of

Pentecostalism. Fayetteville: University of Arkansas Press, 1988.

Gordon Lindsay, JOHN G. LAKE-APOSTLE TO AFRICA (1981)

Guillermo Maldonado, Divine Encounter with the Holy Spirit (United State of America: Whitaker House, 2017)

Heroes of the 20th Century Church, in Triumphant March, Vol. 1, No. 2. © 2012 – 2017, Jennifer Nkem-Eneanya.

Ironsi John, There Was A Church, A call for great awakening (Nigeria: Ikonicxp, 2017.)

Jackson, Jason. "Miracles in the Book of Acts." ChristianCourier.com. Access date: January 18, 2018. https://www.christiancourier.com/articles/1197-miracles-in-the-book-of-acts

John G. Lake, The Complete Collection of His Life Teachings, Compiled by Roberts Liardon, Whitaker House Publishers (1999)

Knox, John. The History of the Reformation in Scotland. Charles J. Guthrie, ed. Reprint, Edinburgh, Scotland: The Banner of Truth Trust, 1982.

Kenneth Copeland, JOHN G. LAKE: HIS LIFE, HIS SERMONS, HIS BOLDNESS OF FAITH

Liardon, Roberts. Maria Woodworth-Etter: The Complete Collection of Her Life Teachings.

(Tulsa: Albury Publishing, 2000).

Mosy U. Madugba, On Fire For God (Nigeria: Spiritual Life Publication, 2010)

Parham, Charles F. A Voice Crying in the Wilderness. (Baxter Springs, Kan.: Apostolic Faith Bible College; originally published in 1902; 2d ed. in 1910.)

Parham, Sarah E. The Life of Charles F. Parham, Founder of the Apostolic Faith Movement.

(Baxter Springs, Kan.: Apostolic Faith Bible College, 1930.)

Paul Enenche, Go in this thy Might! Six Secrets of Supernatural Power (Nigeria: Destiny Prints and publishers Ltd, 2012.)

P. G Chappell, International Dictionary of Pentecostal and Charismatic Movements 2002.

Reinhard Bonnke: The man who changed the face of Christianity in Africa". BBC. 2019-12-18. Retrieved 2019-12-27.

Roberts Liardon, God's General, why they succeeded and why they some failed (Nigeria:

Evangel Publishers Ltd, 1998.)

Roberts Liardon, God's General, the roaring reformers (Nigeria: Evangel Publishers Ltd, 2003.)

Roberts Liardon, JOHN G. LAKE: THE COMPLETE COLLECTION OF HIS LIFE TEACHINGS

Stanley H. Frodsham, With Signs Following (Springfield, Mo.: Gospel Publishing House, 1941)

Wayne E. Warner, The Woman Evangelist, The Life and Times of Charismatic Evangelist Maria B. Woodworth-Etter (Metuchen, N.J.: The Scarecrow Press, Inc., 1986.)

Wayne Warner, Maria Woodworth-Etter and the Early Pentecostal Movement: A Powerful Voice in the Vanguard of Pentecostalism.

W. T. Stead, The Story of the Welsh Revival, (New York: Fleming H. Revell, 1905).

OBITUARY OF UNCLE PRAYER

If we must continuously have divine visitations, prayer is the first thing, the second thing, the third thing necessary.

Luke 9:28-33
"About eight days later Jesus took Peter, John, and James up on a mountain to pray.

And as he was praying, the appearance of his face transformed, and his clothes became dazzling white.

Suddenly, two men, Moses and Elijah, appeared and began talking with Jesus.

They were glorious to see. And they were speaking about his exodus from this world, which was about to be fulfilled in Jerusalem.

Peter and the others had fallen asleep. When they woke up, they saw Jesus' glory and two men standing with him.

As Moses and Elijah were starting to leave, peter, not even knowing what he was saying, blurted out, "Master, it's wonderful for us to be here! Let's make three shelters as memorials- one for you, one for Moses, and one for Elijah."

Nothing can take the place of prayer if any church or Christian must survive this end time hits from our archenemy.

Our master took few of his disciples to the mountain to pray.

One major reason our churches in some quarters are now ichabod centres is because of the death of uncle prayer.
Don't expect the move of heaven hosts in your life or church if you obituary uncle prayer.

In some quarters, uncle prayer has long been dead and buried.

Divine encounter can't be faked or copied... Don't expect encounter divine upon your life or upon members of your congregation if you don't visit mountain of prayer.

Preaching can be boring if uncle prayer is declared dead. I have been there before.

Christian life is stressful and full of struggles as long as uncle prayer is the mortuary.

Is you prayer life in cold room? Please answer.
Oh lord help!

Please uncle prayer; wake up in our lives, families and churches.

WHOLELIFE MINISTRIES INTERNATIONAL

If you are longing for a connection with people who are passionate about God's Presence, Glory and Power, you have found it!

WLMI is a family, a portion of the household of the Lord, made up of people whose heart is to see nations touched by the Fire of God and to see God's power and glory manifest on this earth like never before.

With a mandate from God our strategy is to go to towns and cities, and to light the Fire of God in the hearts of hungry and willing people and in the process light the fires of revival that will see the Glory of God poured out on this earth and the end-time harvest coming in.

We are on the move to make sure under God, that there will be nowhere and no one devoid of the true and delightful knowledge of God, Who is the source of all life, truth and joy.

We are committed to chart for an authentic, personal and universal knowledge of God in our time and the time to come. This is not mere knowledge about God, but a relational knowledge about Him just as when you are in the sea, water is all around you.

"For the earth shall be filled with the knowledge of the glory of the Lord, as the waters cover the sea" Habakkuk 2:14

More than ever before, the time has come for the church to demonstrate the Word and power of God to a dying world.

OUR MISSION
To preach and teach the whole Gospel of Jesus Christ and be actively involved in the spreading of the Gospel of Jesus Christ. (Matthew 28:18-20)

OUR VISION
To operate a ministry in power and authority that will impact the Fire, Presence and Glory of God to the ends of the earth.

OUR GOAL
To have at least a passionate man in every family of the earth that manifests God's Power, Glory and Holiness.

For information contact us at:
WHOLE LIFE MINISTRIES INTERNATIONAL

E-mail:
wholelifeministries2018@gmail.com
Or ironsijohnmania1@yahoo.com
Phone: +234-7038941093, +234-9074666693